SKATING
on
THIN ICE

SKATING
on
THIN ICE

Anatol Rapoport

RDR Books
Oakland, California

Skating on Thin Ice

RDR Books
4456 Piedmont
Oakland, CA 94611
Phone: (510) 595-0595
Fax: (510) 595-0598
E-mail: read@rdrbooks.com
Website: www.rdrbooks.com

ISBN 1-57143-084-9

Library of Congress Catalog Card Number 2001096154

Editors: Bob Drews and Joanna Pearlman
Text Design and Typography: Richard Harris
Cover Design and Production: Jennifer Braham
Title Consultant: Jonathan Rapoport
Cover Art: Marc Chagall, "La Fenêtre,"
© 2001 Artists Rights Society, (ARS), New York/ADAGP, Paris

Distributed in Canada by General Distribution Service,
325 Humber College Boulevard, Toronto, Ontario M9W 7C3

Distributed in England and Europe by Airlift Book Company,
8 The Arena, Mollison Avenue, Enfield, Middlesex, England EN37NJ

Distributed in Australia and New Zealand by Astam Books pty Ltd.,
57-61 John Street Liechardt, New South Wales 2038

Printed in Canada

Dedicated to my meshpukhe

CONTENTS

Ukraine and the Black Sea region

FOREWORD

BY ROGER RAPOPORT

IN 1921, WHEN HE WAS 10 YEARS OLD, Anatol Rapoport, my cousin once removed, left Russia with his family for Poland. The story of his escape has been part of my family's folklore for as long as I can remember.

In 1997, my cousin Leonard told me that Anatol was writing his biography. A Russian version of it was published in 1999, and an English translation appeared the following year. On a visit to Toronto I asked Anatol directly whether the remarkable story of his escape was true. He told me it was partly true, partly fiction, and in the process of telling the true story, he mentioned another bit of folklore—a legend of a whole people, not just a family. He was referring to the "Promised Land" and what that legend became in modern times.

Anatol lives with his wife, Gwen, in Wychwood Park, a Toronto neighborhood of 55 stately homes around a pond. In 1999, he was almost as old as the century. In fact, as he told me, his autobiography begins like this: "We are approaching the end of the century, and I am approaching the end of my life. Time to take stock." The near coincidence of Anatol's life with the 20th century is mentioned in the foreword to the Russian edition of his autobiography by a member of the Russian Academy of Sciences. Anatol gave me a translation of that foreword. It reads in part:

> The outstanding scientist, our compatriot Anatol
> Rapoport, was born in Russia and after the October

Revolution found himself abroad with his parents. A celebrated philosopher, psychologist and mathematician, specialist in mathematical biology, he made a major contribution to the development of operationalism, of the theory of games applied to psychology, as well as to the development of general semantics and of general system theory.

As I listened to Anatol telling how he "found himself abroad" after the October Revolution, I wondered whether he paid proper homage to what I belived was the most important event in his life—escaping from Russia by skating across the frozen river that was the border between Russia and Poland. It turned out that there was only a bare mention of it in his autobiography. I decided then and there that a book centered on that episode would delight a large international audience.

Skating on Thin Ice is Anatol's remarkable coming of age story set against the turbulent history of early 20th century Russia. Although his memoir draws from the world of Sholom Aleichem, the Rapoport family lived only briefly in the stetl celebrated in *Fiddler on the Roof*. Anatol's story spans all of southern European Russia from the Caucasus to the Polish border. Written with a keen eye for history in the making, *Skating on Thin Ice* offers the same verisimilitude that is the heart and soul of great Russian fiction. Only this time none of the names have been changed. Powerful scenes, such as illegal passengers disembarking from the roofs and bumpers of freight cars to push an underpowered train uphill, add the sort of detail sure to make a novelist envious. Written with total recall, Anatol's minute by minute account recreates everything except the steam rising from the Zbruch River as he laces his skates.

FATHER GETS A TASTE
OF THE "PROMISED LAND"

Many Russian Jews look to America as the land of milk and honey. But when my father moves to Chicago in 1906 at age 18, his experience is much different.

IN 1906, WHEN HE WAS 18 YEARS OLD, my father, Munia, and his kid brother Niuma went to America. My father didn't want to go, but he had to. Here is why. His father, Naphtali, after whom I was named, died in his 40s of blood poisoning from a rusty nail. His leg was amputated, but it was too late. His family was large, but he had been a good provider and they lived well. From what I know from my uncles and aunts, there were originally 12 or 13 children, but several died early, one boy in a horrible accident. Eight survived—two sisters and six brothers. When their father Naphtali died, life became difficult.

In those days, many Russian Jews looked to America as the "Promised Land." According to a story in the Bible, God promised Abraham, a righteous and pious man, that his descendants would be masters of a bountiful, fertile country.

The Jews were supposedly these descendants, and, indeed, again according to the Bible, when they escaped from Egypt, where they had been slaves for generations, they conquered a part of the territory between Egypt and what is now Lebanon and established a state there. But this land was, in turn, conquered by other warlike peoples, and the Jews were scattered over many countries. Memories of their homeland—the original Promised Land—persisted. Pious Jews continued to believe that one day a savior, the Messiah, would come and would lead them back to the Promised Land. But centuries went by and the Messiah didn't come.

However, a country was born across an ocean, where people from Europe were welcome and where there was opportunity for everyone, including Jews, to make a good living, where there were no humiliating restrictions on where Jews could live, above all no pogroms. The new country across the ocean, the United States of America, became a sort of substitute for the Promised Land—a very attractive substitute, because it actually existed in the present instead of imagined in a vague future.

Not many could scrape up enough money to pay for passage across the ocean. But since most Jews had large families, a way was found. A member of the family who was most likely to find a well-paying job was to go first, as soon as the passage money could be found. Once in America, he or she would get a job and put aside as much money as could be spared to pay for another ticket or two. Then these family members would come and all would work together to save up money for others to come until the family would be reunited.

This is how my father's family was supposed to emigrate. The first to go was my aunt Sophie, second living child, the

4

*Left to right: Uncle Aron (alias Yevgeny), Uncle Niuma,
youngest brother Boris (author's father), Uncle Yania (eldest brother)*

elder of the two daughters. She had a trade—hat maker. As
soon as she saved enough, she sent for her mother (my grandma Fayga) and my aunt Ruth, the youngest child, eight years
old. Next to go were two brothers—my uncle Mendel (the second son) and my uncle Ike (the fourth). There remained now
my uncle Yania (the eldest), uncle Aron, alias Yevgeny (the
third son, I'll explain the alias later), my father Munia (later
Boris), the fifth son, and my uncle Niuma, the youngest son.

But complications arose. My uncle Yania became the bread-
winner when grandpa Naphtali died. But now that most of the
family was in America, Yania didn't have to continue in that
role. Besides, he had a job that was not just drudgery. He liked

it. He was manager of an estate, and he loved farming. He would surely be a farmer, if Jews were allowed to own land, which they were not in czarist Russia. But managing an estate was the next best thing. The brother next in age, who chose to remain in Russia, was uncle Aron. In 1905, in the wake of Russia's defeat in the war against Japan, a revolution broke out in Russia led by industrial workers. There was fighting in the cities. Barricades were built up from turned-over streetcars, rocks torn from pavements, and bricks. These "fortifications" were meant to stop the soldiers and Cossacks sent to beat up strikers and agitators. Uncle Aron fought on one of the barricades, I believe in Odessa. He was severely beaten, his hand crippled for life. The revolution was crushed, but uncle Aron joined the revolutionary underground. He was in no mood to leave Russia.

There remained my father and uncle Niuma. Grandma Fayga insisted that they come to America. Father wasn't particularly enthusiastic about going. He was in love with his cousin Delia, who eventually became my mother. Delia's father, my grandpa Pinchus, and Munia's father Naphtali were brothers. Among Jews, marriages between cousins were permitted, and the Russian government didn't interfere in the religious practices of non-Christians, as long as they were not politically subversive. I don't think my parents were formally engaged at that time, but everyone knew how they felt about each other. However, grandma Fayga insisted that her two youngest sons come, and in that family she was the undisputed ruler even when grandpa Naphtali was alive. So father went and took uncle Niuma with him. They went to Chicago.

I have the 1911 edition of the *Encyclopedia Britannica*. It is, perhaps, the most famous edition of that famous collection. I cherish it because it is exactly as old as I am and because I inherited it from uncle Niuma. Here is an excerpt from it about Chicago, the city where six of my father's family of nine settled.

The city hall and the court house (cost $4,500,500) is an enormous double building in the free French Renaissance style with columned façades. The new Federal building (finished in 1905; cost $4,750,000) is a massive edifice (a low rectangle surmounted by an inner cross and crowned with a dome). The public library (1893-1897, $2,125,000), constructed of dark granite and limestone, with rich interior decorations of varied frescoes, mosaics, ornamental bronze and iron work, and mottoes, is one of the handsomest libraries of the country. The Chicago Art Institute (1892-1893, Italian Renaissance), the Chicago Orchestra building (1904), and the Commercial National Bank are also noteworthy. The finest residence streets are the Lake Shore Drive of the North Side and the "boulevards"—broad parkways that connect the parks of the city, of which Michigan Avenue, Drexel and Grand are the finest.

If the prices of the buildings don't impress you, multiply the dollars by 20, which would reflect their buying power in our time. However, what matters in this story is not how a tourist would see Chicago in 1906 but how my father saw it. It is possible that he saw none of the palatial buildings, none of the boulevards and none of the parks they connected. When he got off the train that carried him from New York, he hoisted the two trunks (his and uncle Niuma's worldly possessions) on one of the horse-drawn wagons waiting for fares and showed the driver a piece of paper with grandma Fayga's address on it. The ride didn't take long. Father's people lived only a mile or two from the station. And this is where he lived for a year.

I don't think father ever wandered more than a few blocks from the neighborhood where Jewish immigrants lived in those days. Maybe I am mistaken. Perhaps he did get away on occasions to wander over the city and see the splendors described in the *Britannica*. But what good did it do? He may as well have seen all those splendid buildings on picture postcards. They didn't become part of his life. And even if he did somehow get to see the paintings and sculptures at the Art Institute or hear a symphony concert or read the books in the Renaissance-style public library, the most beautiful in the country, with whom would he share his thoughts and impressions?

Father's family lived in slums very much like the slums of New York's lower East Side in the early 20th century. The neighborhood was lively enough, as were all the Jewish ghettos of the time. The air was full of sounds—pushcart vendors vocally advertising their wares, the din of quarrelling, women screaming at kids, barrel organ music, drivers shouting at their horses. Maxwell Street in the heart of the neighborhood was an open-air market, where mostly second-hand clothes were sold. The merchants amused themselves by playing pranks on their customers. Father once told me about how shocked he was by these pranks. One merchant was signalling to another across the street to look at a departing customer wearing an ill-fitting coat. He was gloating about how skillfully he "put one over" on the simple-minded customer. Probably the two merchants amused themselves by competing in how far they could go in selling the worst-fitting item.

The stock yards were about three miles to the south. When the wind was from there, the unbearable stench spread all over the city but was especially intense in the ghetto. At the time, the stock yards conferred on Chicago the somewhat morbid title of "the hog butcher of the world." The slaughter and impressively efficient packing of the carcasses on conveyer belts was one of the tourist sights, along with the Renaissance-style Public Library and Art Institute.

All these attractions, the cultural centers, the picturesque life of the ghetto, the celebrated stock yards were of little interest to father. His thoughts were of Russia, where he had already begun to aspire to a "cultured" life of an educated professional or a dedicated revolutionary like his elder brother. And, of course, there were also persistent thoughts about Delia, his blonde cousin.

Almost immediately after his arrival in Chicago, father got a job in a cigar factory. The hours were long, the pay meager, and there was no promotion to look forward to. He did make some friends among the factory workers, young men who spoke Russian or Yiddish, and that made life less oppressive. In time he learned some English but not enough to talk about matters that interested him. This was just as well, because it was mainly with the immigrants from Russia that he was able to talk about such matters—ideas picked up from his brother Aron alias Yevgeny, the revolutionary with the crippled hand.

In short, father got the impression that America, too, had its revolutionaries. They were not like his brother, a budding intellectual, already well educated, being trained for a profession (he eventually became a pharmacist). The revolutionaries in America were largely immigrants, working in mills or factories, where wages were barely enough to live on, working hours long, working conditions often dangerous and usually demeaning. Such premises were appropriately called "sweat shops." Their "revolutionary activity" was not plotting to overthrow the government or throwing bombs at czars or their ministers, as it was in Russia, especially in its early phases. The principal "subversive" activity of the American (or rather Americanized) workers was the organization of labor unions. This activity was harshly and effectively resisted by the bosses. Professional spies were introduced into shops, who reported any activity related to the organization of a union, which led to summary firings of the organizers and their followers or sympathizers.

Father found himself in a quandary. On the one hand, he was one of the breadwinners of the family. To lose his job meant to deprive the family of his help. On the other hand, if he decided to keep his job at any cost, this would mean dissociating himself from the people with whom he had established tight bonds of friendship, firmed by a common cause. It might even mean being under pressure to spy on his fellow workers, the alternative being the loss of his job. He started thinking about getting out of the situation. And of course, thoughts about his cousin persisted and became sharper and more vivid.

Finally he took the plunge. He told his mother about his decision to go back to Russia. Now grandma Fayga was a complicated person. On the one hand, she was strong willed, domineering and almost fanatically religious. One the other hand, she read Russian fluently and was genuinely interested in classical Russian literature. I know this, because father told me she had frequently discussed Tolstoy's and Dostoevsky's novels with him. Since father was only 15 when grandma Fayga and aunt

Ruth left Russia, this means that he was leaning toward things Russian already in adolescence.

I never asked father to explain how the two sides of grandma fitted together. I suspect this was because grandma was a Bershtein (Russian form of Bernstein). Her brothers were well off. Their occupation was managing estates of absentee owners, which my uncle Yania learned from them. So they were educated in Russian and generally "sophisticated." Maybe some of it rubbed off on grandma but had to be concealed, because it was unseemly for a Jewish woman to be interested in worldly matters. And maybe this was why she and father were so close. She could level with him. Anyway, grandma was devastated by father's decision. I suspect that because of his intellectual interests, he was of all her sons closest to her.

Grandma knew that being imperative with father would lead nowhere. She must have entreated him not to leave, but he had made up his mind. Years later, he sobbed bitterly when he was told of her death, as we were already on the way to America.

A THORNY BUT WELL-MARKED PATH

Education is a luxury and privilege in pre-revolution Russia.
For the couple who would become my parents, it is a passion
and a bond.

MY PARENTS BELONGED TO A GENERATION of Russian Jews who
even as teenagers rejected religion and with it much of Jewish
culture. In Eastern Europe, Jewish culture for centuries was
bound up with Jewish religion. Russian Jews who clung to tra-
dition but were not rabbis or Hebrew scholars were restricted
to petty business like peddling old clothes or usable junk or
else they became tailors, cobblers or locksmiths. The most
prestigious of these trades was watchmaker. Many watchmak-
ers were Jews. Respected professions required higher education, and this path to a higher social status was almost closed
to Jews. Even the *gymnasia* (secondary schools, corresponding
to our high schools) were all but barred to Jews. The quota for
Jews was 3 percent. The same quota applied to universities.

Still some made it. It was possible to find a way around the
gymnasia. One could study by oneself. This way to higher edu-

cation was difficult but it was well marked. At all times you knew how far you had gone and how much was left go to. Here is the way it worked. The Russian *gymnasia* had eight classes (grades). The first class corresponded roughly to the fifth grade in the American grade school. The basics, reading, writing and simple arithmetic, were taught in a primary school. However, these primary schools were not available everywhere and, on the whole, were pretty poor. They did not really prepare the children for the *gymnasia*. So parents who wanted their children to go on to middle level or higher education arranged for private tutors for them (if they could afford it). This is the way Jewish children got their primary education if their parents wanted them to be able to read and write Russian and possibly to get into the *gymnasia*.

But there was another way. Exactly the same things were taught in all the *gymnasia* in the Russian Empire, which comprised one-sixth of the world's dry land and stretched over 11 time zones. To see how much land it covered (and the Russian Federation still covers), recall that the continental U.S. stretching all the way across North America has four time zones, while Canada, which is still longer from West to East, stretches over 5 time zones.

Since the programs of study in the Russian *gymnasia* were the same in the whole vast country, so were the textbooks. I remember, in particular, the geography books. Geography was taught in four classes and there was a textbook for each class. The first class textbook was general geography of the earth: climates, some simple explanations of how weather is determined, positions of continents and oceans, the meaning of the equator, latitude, longitude, map reading, etc. The second class textbook was "Asia, Africa, America and Australia." The third was "Europe" and the fourth "Russia." Science textbooks were also uniform throughout the country. There were textbooks on plants ("Botany"), animals ("Zoology"), the human body ("Anatomy") and general science (small bits of physics and chemistry). There were textbooks on history, ancient, medieval and modern, one on Russian history alone. And there was religion, called "God's Law," taught by a priest. All this you had to know to get a "certificate of maturity," which entitled you to apply for admittance to a university (getting in was another matter).

If you studied at home, with tutors or by yourself or maybe with your parents' help, you knew exactly what you had to know. In fact, if you could memorize the textbooks, you would know everything there was to know. When you felt you were ready, you applied to take an examination for many classes of the *gymnasia*. On these examinations, some written, most of them oral, you were asked questions, the answers to which were in the textbooks. If you knew what was in the textbooks and accordingly answered the questions, you passed and were given a certificate for so many classes. Once you passed your examinations for all eight classes you got the coveted "certificate of maturity." It entitled you to apply for admittance in a university. This is what my parents aspired to.

My mother's family lived in Cherkassy, a middle-sized town on the right bank of the Dnieper, the main river flowing into the Black Sea in what is now Ukraine. The family lived in dire poverty. Grandpa Pinchus Rapoport tried out various "lines of business," actually petty trading in whatever came along. Business was terrible. But he kept hoping that things would improve. My mother told me an interesting story about how grandma Ethel readily accepted grandpa's proposal for marriage.

To begin with he was blond. My, mother, the eldest of seven children, was also blond, and so was I, until the little hair I had left turned white. Blondness was a rarity among Jews and, perhaps for that reason seemed attractive to some girls. Perhaps if they knew the probable reason for that rarity, they wouldn't admire it so much. Some think that blond hair among Jews can be traced to revolt of Ukraine against Polish suzerainty in 1648. Ukrainians were Eastern Orthodox Christians like the Russians, while the Poles were Roman Catholics. There were persistent attempts on the part of the Polish clergy to convert Ukrainians to Roman Catholicism. Bogdan Khmelnitsky, the leader of the revolt, hated the Jews even more than Roman Catholics. Some among the Jews were agents of Polish officialdom (tax collectors, etc.). A storm of pogroms swept over the Ukraine. Rape was as common as murder. So blond hair appeared among some Jewish children and passed on to succeeding generations.

However, grandpa's blondness was not the main attraction. What appealed to grandma Ethel was that grandpa was a "modern" young man. He came to woo grandma himself instead of sending a matchmaker, which was traditional among Jews at that time. But what attracted grandma most was that he wore a European business suit instead of the traditional long black coat. Moreover, except for a mustache, he was clean shaven. "Exotic" is the word that comes to mind. But, as I said, as a "freelance" businessman, grandpa was not a success. Kids came one after the other, and poverty tightened its grip. Grandma started to take in borders, but that was a losing proposition. She had even less business sense than grandpa. She thought of the borders as if they were her children and was according-ly recklessly generous in the meals she served.

So when in adolescence my mother showed symp-toms of aspiration to a secu-lar education, this did not meet with sympathy, espe-cially with grandpa. The generation gap that devel-oped among the Russian

Author's mother

Jews during the first decade of the century was very much like the generation gap that developed in succeeding generations of many cultures (including, as we know, among Americans). Grandpa was quick-tempered. Emotional scenes ensued. Grandpa's "modernity" dissipated. Once he discovered a pic-ture postcard of Venus of Milo among mother's possessions The goddess, bare to her hips, was the last straw. Grandpa confis-cated it and forbade mother to associate with gentiles. (Her best friend, Raya, of whom she often spoke, was Christian.) Mother left home and went to Kiev.

Kiev was then the third-largest city in Russia. It had a uni-versity, museums, libraries, theaters, a respectable opera house—all the amenities of "culture." Mother thought she might be able to enroll in a *gymnasium*. I don't know how she expected to live. I know we had distant relatives there. Perhaps

17

they helped her. Of course, she was not admitted. She even had no right to live in Kiev. The only Jews allowed to live in large cities were qualified professionals and those with specified skills. I suspect mother lived with these distant relatives who prudently omitted to register her, so that her presence in Kiev was unknown to the authorities. However, fortune smiled on her. A couple of elderly spinsters (sisters) who were teachers in a *gymnasia* undertook to tutor her free of charge. Possibly they were impressed by a youngster's ambition to get an education and were sufficiently kind hearted to do something about it.

In this way, Delia, my father's beloved, embarked on that thorny (but well-marked) path—the path to a certificate of maturity—studying "externally" and passing examinations one by one until an examination on the curriculum of all eight classes was passed.

By our standards, the two nice ladies were neither very competent nor inspiring teachers. But they were just the sort of teachers that could well prepare an "external" student for the examinations. To be prepared meant to know the "right" answers to questions that could be asked at an examination. So when mother came for her lesson, she recited (in her own words or, sometimes, literally, if she didn't understand what she read) the paragraphs or pages assigned to her as "home work." Later she used to amuse friends by reciting in a quick patter "the peninsulas of North America": "Alaska, California, Yucatan, Florida, Labrador!" (It was required to name them counterclockwise.) I remember mother saying that she thought Florida and Labrador were very much alike because they had so many letters in common and were pronounced in the same breath.

On another occasion she was to recite something from

18

Greek mythology. It went something like this: "The gates of Hades were guarded by a fierce dog, named Kerberus."

"Cerberus, my dear," one of the ladies gently corrected her.

Mother ventured to object. "In my book, it says Kerberus."

"Really?" said the teacher. "Let me see it. Why so it is— Kerberus. But this must be an old edition."

Quite likely. Mother may have bought it in the flea market. "And I never found out," mother continued her story, "whether the dog was 'Kerberus' or 'Cerberus,' nor what or where this Hades was. Maybe the information was in the books, but it is also possible that the good ladies forgot to mark the passage as part of the assignment."

On the whole, mother made pretty good progress on the way to the certificate of maturity. But she didn't make it. She got sick—acute appendicitis. So she returned home to Cherkassy crestfallen. But she didn't give up yet. She met my father, whom she hadn't seen since childhood. Now she saw her 17-year-old cousin in quite a different light. They fell in love. Both of them at once. Deep love. Aside from the usual personal attraction, they both had the same ambition—to get a secular education, to make it to the university or to an "insti- tute," as post-secondary schools for women were called, to get a profession, to be able to live in a city, in short to get kul- turnost. They were going to tread the "thorny, well-marked path" hand-in-hand.

Since they were cousins, there was no objection to their spending time together alone. So whatever else they did, they studied. Father was considerably ahead, having got the bug when he was still going to *heder*. So in the process of studying, he played the part of a tutor for mother, which helped both of them. Inevitably, the nature of their relationship was noticed, but both grandma Ethel and grandpa Pinchus approved, and while Delia and Munia were not formally engaged, there was an understanding. The urgent plea from grandma Fayga from Chicago was a cruel blow. But I have already told how it was averted. Father went, feeling the obligation of taking his kid brother across, stayed a year, and in spite of his mother's entreaties came back.

CHAPTER

3

I JOIN MY PARENTS

*I am born in 1911 in the industrial town of Lozovaya and
given the name Anatoli even though the official rabbi tells my
mother "There is no such name." I know only 3 years of life
before World War I changes everything.*

MY PARENTS WERE MARRIED on March 19, 1910, by the Julian calendar, which was in use in Russia until after the revolution and
which is still used by the Russian Orthodox Church. After the
revolution, the Gregorian calendar, now used all over the
world, replaced it. All dates were moved 13 days forward. So
by our reckoning, Boris and Adel Rapoport (as they now called
themselves) were married on April 1, 1910.

I was born on May 22, 1911, by the present calendar, but it
was May 9 by the Julian calendar. May 9 was a national holiday
in czarist Russia because it was the czar's *imianiny* ("name
day"). Orthodox Russians celebrated their "name day" rather
than birthday. Everyone was named after a saint of the Russian
Orthodox Church, and every saint had a date, important saints
more than one. St. Nicholas was an important saint (in fact,

Santa Claus is a corruption of his name) so he has two "name days": one in December, the other on May 9 (by the Julian calendar). The czar's name was Nicholas (Nicholas II); so on the morning of the day I was born (at 3 a.m.) all the church bells in Lozovaya were ringing. Boris and Adel were not Orthodox Christians, but they often told me about this bell ringing and how good they felt about it.

My mother's parents and siblings moved to the town of Lozovaya when my father was in America, and that was the town to which he came back. Its status was not clear. I say "status" because everything and everyone in czarist Russia had a status, which ranged from the highest to the lowest. For example, every person had an official status. The person with the highest status of all was, of course, the czar, officially called "Autocrat of all the Russias." Then came the royal family, then the titled nobility (princes, counts, barons), *dvorianie* (the gentry, people of "noble birth," but without titles), then *grazhdanie* (the "citizens") and *meshchanie* ("burghers," people of humble birth but living in towns rather than villages). At the bottom were the *krestianie* ("peasants"), who lived in villages. Practically all Jews were *meshchanie*, the next to the lowest class. But if they got a higher education, they automatically became *grazhdanie* and could live legally in major cities. That was another incentive to Jews to get a secular education.

Settlements were also assigned a status. The highest status was assigned to the two capitals—St. Petersburg, the site of the Royal Palace and of all the ministries, and Moscow, the ancient capital, where the czars were crowned and buried. Next were *gubernias* (capitals, roughly corresponding to state capitals in the U.S), then *uyezds*, (chief towns corresponding to American

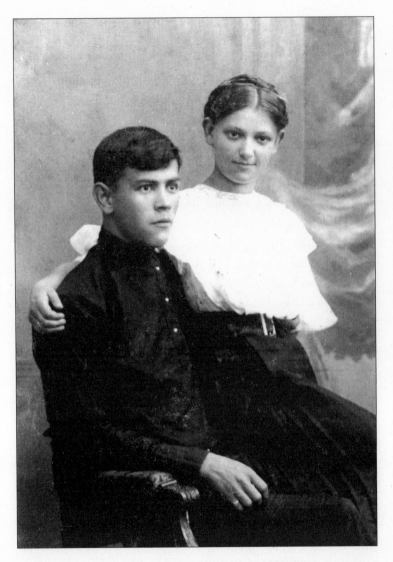

Author's parents as newlyweds

county seats, and which had courthouses and *selos* (towns without administrative institutions but with markets and churches). On the bottom were villages, where peasants lived. These had no government offices and no businesses, except taverns, where peasants could get drunk.

The status of Lozovaya was not clear because it was not officially listed in any of those categories. It was an industrial town (population 14,000, which at that time was substantial) and a railway junction, the intersection of a line going from Moscow south to the Crimea and one from Poltava (a *gubernia*) in the west to the heavily industrialized Donetz Basin in the east. Maybe Lozovaya was slated to be promoted to an *uyezd*, and maybe for that reason it had two *gymnasias*, one for boys and one for girls, even though only towns on the *uyezd* level and above rated a *gymnasia*. This anomaly was of crucial importance to my mother's family. Three of her four sisters and the younger brother all made it into the *gymnasia*, got their certificates of maturity and after the revolution went on to universities. All four became doctors.

The existence of *gymnasias* in Lozovaya was of crucial importance also to my parents, since it enabled them to make a modest but adequate living when they got married. Although neither of them had a *gymnasia* diploma, they had an excellent reputation as tutors. They ran a sort of private school, preparing children to start out on the "thorny but well-marked path" to the certificate of maturity, that is, to a "cultured" professional life. When I was not yet 3, I was often allowed to sit in these classes, having learned that the price to be paid for this privilege was maintaining absolute silence.

Russian Jews who aspired to professional life and adopted

Russian as their language invariably "russified" their names, just as they "anglicized" them in America. My uncle Mendel became Emanuel, uncle Isak became Ike. My father's Hebrew name was Hayim-Bear. He dropped the Hayim and changed Bear into the Russian Boris. My mother's Hebrew name was Hanna-Hoodle. She dropped the "Hanna" and changed "Hoodle" into Adel (Delia is the diminutive form). The change from Aron to Yevgeny cannot be explained this way, but this was probably connected to my uncle's underground revolutionary activity.

In America anyone can adopt a new name and make it official without any trouble. In czarist Russia, this was by no means the case. The "russified" version of the Hebrew name was tolerated as an informal pseudonym, pen name, stage name and the like, but the Hebrew name remained in the passport (which everyone in the Russian empire had to possess) and used in all official business, in court, and so on.

When I was born, my birth certificate had to be made out by the official rabbi. This functionary was not a "rabbi" in the Jewish sense (someone who was either a religious minister or thoroughly learned in Hebrew religious and philosophical literature). The official rabbi was the liaison person between the Jewish community and the Russian government. Among his duties were making out birth and death certificates, issuing marriage licenses and so on.

So when my mother came to the official rabbi to register my birth, he asked the usual question: "Child's name?"

"Anatoli," said my mother. The official rabbi was puzzled. "There is no such name," he said. "Whom was he named after?"

"He was named after his deceased grandfather Naphtali," said mother.

"Then I will register him under this name. He was circumcised, wasn't he?"

"He was, but you will do no such thing. You will register him as A-na-to-li."

And she spelled it out in Hebrew letters. She had him there, because there is no Jewish law that restricts given names. The Bible is full of instances where children were named by some word commemorating an event or whatever.

And Leah conceived, and bore a son, and she called his name Reuben; for she said, "Behold the Lord hath looked upon my affliction; for now my husband will love me." (Genesis 29: 32.)

There was more to this Anatoli business. When I was about a year old, I grew several angiomas. These are benign enlargements of blood vessels that appear on various parts of the body, usually no bigger than large pimples. As a rule they can be easily removed by passing an electric current through them or freezing them. I had one on my back and one on my scalp, and these were easily removed. The third one, however, was on my left eyelid and grew to the size of a small cherry. No surgeon wanted to take a chance of freezing or cauterizing it for fear of damaging the eye. Mother took me to cities where competent surgeons were practicing and finally found one in Kharkov. Dr. Trinkler was his name. He told mother that he thought of a way to remove the angioma from my eyelid. It seems it hadn't been done before, but it was worth trying. He said he would tie up the blood vessels that fed the tumor's growth. It worked. In a couple of weeks, the angioma fell off. Only a scar remained.

26

I was going to connect this to the Anatoli business. There was an incident in Dr. Trinkler's office. The receptionist was taking down the data, and in answer to the question of what my name was, mother said "Anatoli." The receptionist looked severely at her. "What is his *Hebrew* name?" she asked. Mother kept her cool. She said slowly, but emphatically, "A-na-to-li." The receptionist raised her voice. Dr. Trinkler happened to come

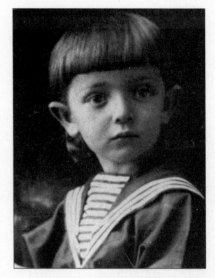

Author aged three

in and asked the receptionist what was the matter. The receptionist explained. Then mother explained. Dr. Trinkler turned to the receptionist: "Didn't you hear? The child's name is Anatoli. Kindly register him as such." Then to mother, "I have a little Anatoli, too."

My earliest recollections take me back to before my third birthday. My favorite toy was a set of little wooden blocks, shaped like bricks. I would stack them up to see how tall a "tower" I could build before they toppled. Or else I would arrange them in different patterns. I was very fond of them. Then, somehow, they got lost. Mother couldn't find another set in the one toy store we had in Lozovaya. She bought me a set of blocks instead with letters on them. Soon I learned all the letters of the Russian alphabet. Father even showed me how to put p—a—p—a side by side and to "read" the word.

Along with learning to read, I pretended to write. I always made the same pattern with a pencil:

VVVVVVVVVVVVVVVVVVVVVVVV

As I said earlier, father and mother kept a sort of a private school, preparing children for the *gymnasia*. Once, during a recess, a youngster asked me what I was doing. I said, "I'm writing, can't you see?"

"That's not proper writing," he said. And I said, "I'm writing in German." Thereupon the boy took my pencil, wrote a great big capital J in Gothic script and said, "Now *there's* a German letter." I was impressed.

On my third birthday, the church bells were ringing as usual to mark the czar's name day, and I was allowed for the first time to cross the street *alone* to the house where grandpa and grandma lived. I barged in shouting, "I came alone! I'm 3 years old!"

That was in spring 1914, the last spring before World War I. What I remember most vividly is that uncle Niuma (who had gone to America with father and stayed there) was visiting. He came to register for military service (which all men in Russia had to do every year), because he didn't want to lose his Russian citizenship. Like father, whom he adored, he was not favorably impressed by the "Promised Land."

I remember young uncle Niuma as a jolly, fun-loving, happy-go-lucky character. I loved to see him do imitations of Charlie Chaplin and hear him sing American popular songs. One of them went like this: "Any little girl, who's a *nice* little girl is the *right* little girl for me!" He would bounce me on his knee as he sang it and would explain what the words meant.

"But I'm not a little girl," I would say, "I'm a boy." "Let's pretend you're a little girl," uncle Niuma would say, and I thought it was terribly funny. I became very fond of him. On one occasion, he showed me an airplane flying over the town. That was a rarity in those days. Everyone turned out to watch.

He went back to Chicago just a few weeks before World War I started. My uncle Misha, the elder of mother's two brothers, was not so fortunate. He had already been inducted into the army and when the war broke out was immediately sent to the Austrian front. Fortunately for him, he was taken prisoner almost immediately and so was able to "sit out" the war in an Austrian prisoner-of-war camp. Also, my father was able to keep out of both World War I and the civil war that raged in Russia from 1918 to 1921. Nevertheless, 1914, when my fourth year began, was a prominent steppingstone in my life.

FATHER ESCAPES THE DRAFT

My father has a system for escaping the draft. As the carnage of war spreads, he is probably escaping a death sentence.

Everyone in a certain age group in Russia had to be in the military even in peacetime. The only way to get out was to fail the physical exam.

FROM WHAT I WROTE about Jews in czarist Russia, it should be clear that they didn't love the czarist regime enough to fight and kill for it. So as a rule they tried hard to get out of military service. Father managed to flunk it year after year. Several weeks before he went to register, he starved himself, I mean *really* starved himself. Actually, he was always thin. But when he came to take his physical he was about 30 pounds underweight, and that was that. The verdict was "unfit." And he was safe for another year. Safe from serving three years in the army, war or no war.

Army service in czarist Russia was a terrible ordeal. Recruits were abused by corporals and sergeants, often savagely beaten.

Some were assigned as servants to officers who were as quick as the drill sergeants to resort to brutal beatings. So when a Jew flunked his physical, there was usually a joyous family celebration. Father "broke his fast" at one of these celebrations and for the next several weeks ate and ate and ate until he restored his normal weight. Year after year the whole business was repeated.

Every time father registered for the draft and failed his physical he was given a card that specified the "category" in which he was put. These categories classified the young men in accordance with "degree of fitness."

In 1914 Russia went to war. In the first weeks, the invasion of East Prussia, a province of the German empire, was successful. The papers were full of "hurrah for our side" shouting, predictions of an early end of the war and stuff like that. But the Germans' retreat was a ruse. They enticed the Russians to advance rapidly, thus stretching their lines so that supplies could no longer follow them. Then the Germans attacked with heavy artillery and armored cars (which the Russian peasants had never seen). Two Russian armies were destroyed. The commander of one committed suicide.

There was a similar fiasco on the Austrian front in the south. Initially the Russians advanced rapidly into Galicia, just across the border of the Austrian-Hungarian empire. Again they outran their supply trains. German troops were thrown into the battle to help the Austrians, who were always rather indifferent warriors, and rescued them.

That was where my uncle Misha (mother's brother) was lucky. He was taken prisoner and so was safe for the duration. By then the shortage of men to be thrown into the slaughter became severe. Even those in the exempt categories were called up for immediate service. This included my father. Again he managed to avoid being drafted.

When the directive came that men in father's category were to report immediately, it was printed on posters and pasted on walls, fences, etc., all over towns. Few people read newspapers, since 80 percent of Russian peasants were illiterate. Among townspeople perhaps 60 percent couldn't read. But illiteracy didn't help them. They didn't have to read the posters to know what they were about. The news spread like wildfire, so everyone was assumed to know that they couldn't leave town.

It so happened that father was acquainted with the only printer in town, who was to print the posters and have them posted. This printer did father a favor that may have saved his life. He told him about the posters the day before they were to be put up. So it was still possible to take the train and leave. Father lost no time packing. He went to Baku in the Caucasus. His elder brother (the revolutionary) was living there under an assumed name with a forged passport. That's why he was known as Yevgeny instead of Aron.

The Caucasus, with Baku the largest city, was conquered by Russia during the 19th century. People of many different nationalities lived there: Armenians, Georgians, Circassians, Chechens, Azerbaijani, Persians, Turks. The Armenians and Georgians were Christians, but practically all the others were Moslems. Turkey is also predominantly a Moslem country, and in World War I, Turkey was an ally of Germany. So when Germany declared war on Russia and vice versa, Russia also declared war on Turkey. On this front the Russians couldn't trust the Moslems to fight against their fellow Moslems in Turkey. Quite possibly many would desert and join the other side. Most of them hated the Russian conquerors of the Caucasus. For this reason Russia didn't venture to draft the men of the Caucasus in the war against Turkey. So father was safe. This made up in some measure for the grief that struck my mother. I was only 4, but already strongly attached to my father, so I also felt his absence keenly. It was from this time on (early fall of 1915) that my memories are more or less continuous, not just unconnected happenings.

CHAPTER

5

WE MOVE IN WITH MOTHER'S FAMILY

I grow up in Lozovaya in some luxury by Russian standards.
Grandpa has a modest house with a little orchard that fills me
with memories I keep to this day. I love my grandpa. He shows
me Hebrew letters and tells me stories and fairy tales.

BY THE TIME FATHER RETURNED FROM AMERICA in 1907, grandpa
Pinchus and his family had moved to Lozovaya, the town where
I was born. This Lozovaya is considerably farther east than
Cherkassy, where the family had lived and where mother and
her siblings were born. The surrounding land was a rich wheat
country, blessed with the famous Ukrainian *chornoziom* (very
fertile black soil). Grandpa became a purveyor of wheat. As far
as I know, this meant that he bought harvested wheat from the
peasants and delivered it to central storage areas. The profits
from these sales were his living, in fact a pretty good living.

Grandpa Pinchus was no longer poor. So he built a house. It
was finished in 1911, the year of my birth. It was a one-story
house. There was a small porch. The front door had a bell to

ring. It was not an electric bell (there was no electricity), but you twisted something, and it rang. There was also a large double gate, crowned by a grill with "1911" on it. When both halves were opened, a carriage could go into the yard behind the house. The yard was where chickens ran about looking for crumbs, grains of wheat or millet seed. There was also an entrance to a cellar, which served as an ice box. In winter it was packed with ice, which lasted through the summer.

The kitchen door opened on this yard. On the opposite side were lean-tos used as storage places. In fall during the festival of *Sukkoth,* commemorating the nomadic era when Jews lived in tents, it was customary to sleep outside one's house. Grandpa and grandma and perhaps some of their children slept in those lean-tos during the *Sukkoth* festival. I thought it was great fun.

There was also a small orchard with several cherry trees, an apple tree and a pear tree. There was also a peach tree, which bore no fruit since the climate was not right for it. Also there were berry-bearing bushes—currants, raspberries and gooseberries. In late summer the berries were gathered and made into preserves that lasted through the winter. There was also a rose bush. Grandma made rose jam out of petals, which was my favorite.

The house itself was quite respectable, a sort of middle-class house by the standards of the time in Russia (but not in America). There was no plumbing, that is no running water and no flush toilets. Bathing was in a tub placed in the kitchen. There was a privy with two booths. In winter, chamber pots were used and emptied into the privies. The stuff was collected and carted away in wagons. When such a wagon appeared in a street, pedestrians shouted "*Vezut!*" ("It's coming!") and took cover.

There was no electricity either. In the evening, kerosene lamps were lit. They were regarded as luxury, more "civilized" than candles. Peasants didn't have even candles. They burned *luchinas* (dry sticks).

From the front door you entered a corridor, the left wall of which was all windows. It must have been a southern exposure, since there was a lot of sunshine in the corridor. The door to the interior was on the right. Through it you entered a vestibule with three doors. To the left was a bedroom, for some reason called nursery, although the youngest (beside myself) was already 14. When we moved in, mother and I slept there and also aunt Rose, the eldest of mother's sisters (mother was the eldest). The door to the right led to the parlor. This room was intended to be for show only, but during the war roomers lived in it. The parlor had two armchairs, a sofa, potted plants, etc. In the vestibule, the door straight ahead led into the dining room, which served also as a living room. In the evening grandpa and grandma and their guests (who came frequently) sat around the table and talked—very loudly and with much laughter.

From this dining-living room a door led into the kitchen, which was large and contained two ovens. One was a Russian oven *(pech),* a sort of cave with clay walls. Bread was baked in that oven. Also food that was to be kept hot, for instance food cooked Friday for the Sabbath, since no fire could be lit on the Sabbath. The other oven was a *plita*. On top of it were burners, something like the burners on our gas or electric ranges. The *plita* was heated by wood. Food was boiled or fried on these burners.

Above the *plita* and behind the *pech* was a place to sleep. It was always warm, even hot in winter when there was fire in the *plita* or in the *pech*. In peasant hovels, the top of the oven was a luxurious place to sleep. Usually the old man of the family (no longer working) slept and spent his time in this alcove, while the family slept on *polati* (planks covered with bags filled with straw or something like that). In grandpa's house the peasant girl who helped with the housework slept on the *pech*. Everyone else slept in beds or on couches. There was one master bedroom off the dining-living room, where grandma and grandpa slept in twin beds, as was customary.

There was also a separate apartment: a large room and a large kitchen with a *plita* but no *pech*.

My two youngest aunts, Esia and Pasha, slept on a couch in the living room. This left uncle Borya and aunt Tsina. Possibly one of them slept in the parlor, on the sofa, the other in the apartment.

Water came from a well on our street. It had to be boiled, since it probably teemed with microbes. Much tea was drunk throughout the day. Hardly anyone drank water. Water for tea was boiled in a *samovar,* which means self-boiler. People who scoffed at Russia's technological backwardness called the *samovar* the only Russian invention. It was a tall brass cylinder. Inside of it was a pipe coated with clay. When water was poured in, it surrounded that pipe. The upper end of the pipe was narrower, so that the pipe had a shoulder near the top. Eggs could be laid on this shoulder to be boiled. The vessel was heated by charcoal dropped into the pipe. The heat also boiled the eggs, which could be marked and taken out at different times, so that some would be soft boiled, some medium boiled, some hard boiled.

The whole point of this "invention" was that the water could be kept nearly boiling for a long time, sometimes hours, depending on the size of the *samovar.* This made tea drinking an established social occasion. The *samovar* would occupy the place of honor at one end of the table. The hostess would usually preside. Her duty was to ask each guest whether he/she preferred "strong," "medium" or "weak" tea, lemon or cream. Then she would pour the brewed tea from a tea pot that rested on top of the whole contrivance, in which the brewed tea would stay hot. After pouring the proper amount of brewed tea into the guest's glass (not cup), she put the glass underneath a little faucet on the *samovar's* belly to fill the glass. Finally she added lemon or cream and passed the glass to the guest. During the course of the session (at which lively conversation was always held), a guest might drink as many as 10 glasses, depending, of course, on the number of guests and the size of the *samovar.*

Everyone loved to drink tea—Russians, Ukrainians, Jews. As I said, tea drinking was a social occasion, but not a genteel one, as in England, where in high society teacups were said to be held with the bent little finger sticking out. That's why tea has been traditionally regarded in America as a sissy drink. Could you imagine a cowboy on the range drinking tea out of a cup instead of black coffee out of a can? In Russia, tea was everyone's drink and the *samovar* an object of fondness and respect. It even participated in the conversation by making gentle noises (as steam seeped through its cover). When there was a lull in the conversation, the people listened to its hum. They said the samovar "sings its little song."

There is another reason why I think of the *samovar* with fondness. Jews were not permitted to handle fire in any way on the Sabbath. If it was necessary to do so, a "Sabbath goy" (that is, a gentile doing various chores on Saturday) was asked to help out. A child could also be used. So on Saturday mornings, grandma would always ask me to strike a match and ignite the dry sticks put into the pipe of the *samovar* to ignite the charcoal. It made me feel important.

If you don't count my youngest aunt, Pasha, who was about 14 at the time, I was the only child surrounded by eight adults. It goes without saying that I was doted on, probably spoiled. All of mother's siblings spoke Yiddish to their parents but Russian among themselves. Grandma spoke (besides Yiddish) some Ukrainian, which she spoke to the peasant girl who helped with the housework, and halting Russian, which she spoke to me. I spoke only Russian at the time but soon learned to understand Ukrainian, which grandpa spoke fluently, since he had dealings with peasants. We became very close.

Two activities bound us: grandpa told me stories (that is, his at times bizarre versions of them), and we played a simple card game (of the melding variety) called "Thousand." Scores had to be recorded after each deal, and for that purpose the abacus was used, as everywhere in Russia. Waiters in restaurants carried miniature abacuses to tote up bills until the electronic calculators were introduced. So I learned to use the abacus.

I also loved grandpa's versions of Russian fairy tales. I don't know where or when he got to know them. He knew the one about the fire bird that stole apples from a czar's orchard and the one about the peasant's son who courted a princess. To get her he had to kiss her while she was standing on a balcony by making the horse under him leap to her level. He had three chances, failed the first two but succeeded on the last.

Grandpa also taught me the Hebrew letters. I don't think he had much Hebrew schooling, aside from memorizing prayers. He did tell me a Jewish legend once about the prophet Moses when he was a baby. According to the Bible, Moses was born of Jewish parents when Jews were slaves in Egypt. Some fortune teller told the pharaoh (the king of Egypt) that a Jew soon to be born would be his undoing. So he ordered all male Jewish babies to be killed. To save her newborn son, Moses' mother put him in a basket and set it afloat in the Nile, the great river of Egypt. Once pharaoh's daughter went down to the river to bathe and saw the basket with a baby in it floating among the bulrushes. She brought this baby to the palace with her and Moses was raised in the pharaoh's court.

Already as a baby Moses showed unusual intelligence. The pharaoh's advisers warned him that when the boy grew up, he might be dangerous. So to test the baby's intelligence they placed two vessels in front of him. One contained gold coins, the other glowing coals. The idea was to see which the baby would try to grab. If he went for the coals, that would mean that he was still foolish like any normal baby. But if he went for the gold, this would justify the suspicion that he was precocious and so potentially dangerous. So Moses, being actually precocious, reached for the gold. But his guardian angel saved him. He grabbed the baby's arm and moved it toward the bowl with the burning coals. Moses, instead of grabbing the coins, grabbed a glowing coal and even tried to put it in his mouth. This, grandpa explained, is why Moses had a speech defect (mentioned in the Bible) for the rest of his life.

As far as I remember, this was the only piece of Jewish folklore that grandpa told me in our frequent conversations. So it seems, grandpa had little education. When I mentioned my parents' abandoning religion because of their intense thirst for education, I may have given the impression that remaining true to Judaism meant remaining uneducated. This is not so. The most pious Jews were also usually the most thoroughly educated. But there was no common ground between Jewish education and Russian or European secular education. The most pious Jews were also the most ardent scholars. The Yiddish word for synagogue is *schul*. It is related to the German *Schule* and English "school." In America, a synagogue is often called a temple, but pious Jews don't think of it as a temple. The only temple they recognize is the one built by King Solomon, destroyed by Babylonian conquerors, restored by order of King Cyrus of Persia and destroyed by the Romans in 70 A.D. That temple was supposed to be the home of Jehovah, the god worshipped by Jews. There never was any other temple, and there is none now. A portion of the wall, supposedly of the original temple, still stands in East Jerusalem, and pious Jews pray facing that wall.

Jewish education started in the *heder*. Boys began by learning the Hebrew alphabet. Next they learned to read the Torah, the first five books of the Old Testament. At first the *melamed* (teacher) read it to them as they looked at the text. He translated sentence by sentence into Yiddish. The boys were in school all day, perhaps eight hours. So in this way, simply listening to the *melamed* reading Hebrew sentences followed by Yiddish translations, they were supposed to learn Hebrew.

After *heder,* study could be continued in higher institutions of Hebrew learning, These were located in big cities of Poland or Lithuania, countries incorporated into the Russian Empire but free of residence restrictions affecting Jews. Few could afford to go there. The young Jews, who were determined to continue learning, studied by themselves in the synagogue, which usually had a full library of Hebrew classical, that is, basically religious literature.

I, too, had an appetite for learning as far back as I can remember. I liked especially to learn new words I heard in the conversations of the adults and wanted very much to understand them. But I didn't want to betray my ignorance by asking what they meant. So I thought up a way of getting around it. I would memorize two words and would ask "What is the difference between ... and ... ?" When the words were related, this ruse sometimes worked. But once I asked, "What is the difference between 'minimum' and 'notary public'?" And that caused confusion. "Don't you mean the difference between 'minimum' and 'maximum'?" they said. "No," I insisted, "I mean between 'minimum' and 'notary public'." It didn't work. I abandoned the method.

The first "academic" subject I got involved in was arithmetic. Mother ordered a textbook, and I waited impatiently for it. She kept calling the book *zadachnik*. *Zadacha* means "problem" in Russian. *Zadachnik* is a somewhat informal word for "problem book." Maybe that's what the Kiev ladies called it when mother studied with them. So I was eagerly waiting for the arrival of the *zadachnik*. It finally came. As I said, I could read, but mostly simple words that appeared in my little folk tale books. The title of the *zadachnik* was imposing: *Sbornik arifmeticheskikh zadach* ("Collection of Arithmetic Problems"). I finally figured it out syllable by syllable, asked what it meant, which mother explained. I was duly impressed.

This formidable title of a primer shows how solemnly education was regarded in Russia. You can get an idea of the scope of this "Collection of Arithmetic Problems" from the first problem in it:

Mother gave her little boy an apple. Later she gave him another apple. How many apples did mother give her little boy?

I thought it was ridiculously simple. But my disappointment dissipated when I looked at problems in the last chapter. One, I remember:

A merchant bought 40 *arshins* of black and blue serge. Black serge cost 1 ruble, 20 kopeks; blue serge 1 ruble 80 kopeks per *arshin*. The merchant paid 54 rubles in all. How many arshins did he buy of each kind?

When we got to the problems somewhat more complex than the one with the two apples, mother taught me how to break them up into simpler ones and solve them one by one until the final solution became evident. I loved it. But most of all I loved looking into my aunt Pasha's textbooks and listen to her repeating her lessons out loud, literally memorizing the textbook so as to be able to answer brilliantly in class.

There was Russian history. I remember the opening sentence in the textbook to this day:

Our ancestors were called Slavs. The Slavic tribes tried to establish states but these remained weak and were eventually conquered by larger, stronger states. These, too, were conquered sooner or later. Only the strongest state survived. Eventually it became the great Russian empire.

And this is the way the ruling dynasty was established. The story went on:

For a long time the Slavs fought among themselves, so they were easily conquered by others. Finally they decided to establish order. They sent emissaries to a Varyagi tribe, called "Rus." The emissaries said to the Varyagi, "Our land is great and bountiful. But there is no order in it. Come, be our princes and rule over us." A chieftain named Rurik consented and came to Novgorod with his two brothers. This was the beginning of the Russian state.

There was also ancient history. In it was a picture of the Sphinx still buried to her neck in sand. (That was before the half woman, half cat was dug up). There was a book on "nature study" with pictures. I liked the pictures of flowers. There were two pictures I was afraid to look at: one, sort of dark red, of a man without skin (showing all the muscles labeled); another even more scary, of a human skeleton.

This took up practically all of my time. The only recreation I had was playing with my two cousins. Father's eldest brother, uncle Yania also lived in Lozovaya. We were related both through my father and my mother (both Rapoports) and also through grandma, who was a Babinsky. That wasn't the only connection of Rapoports and Babinskys. Uncle Yania married my grandma's younger sister Fania. Uncle Aron (Yevgeny, the revolutionary) married another of grandma's younger sisters, Aniuta. So it was three Rapoport brothers marrying two Babinsky sisters and their niece (my mother).

6

BAKU

We go to the Caucasus to reunite with my father, who fled to escape the draft. On the way, mother tells me about an incident in Tolstoy's life, while he was traveling by train that makes a deep impression on me. It is in Baku that I fall in love with music.

ONE WINTER MORNING, shortly after we woke up but were still in bed, mother said to me, "We are going far, far away—to the Caucasus."

Then she told me about that country and the gigantic mountains with snow on them the year around. (I had never even seen a hill). The sea with waves breaking against the shore (I had never seen a river). People wearing strange clothes and speaking strange languages.

"Not Russian?" I asked.

"No."

"Not Ukrainian?"

"No."

"Not Yiddish?"

"No."

"I know! German!"

"No, not German either. Some speak Tartar, some Armenian, some Persian. You will see them and hear them speak when we are there."

"So how can we talk to them, if they don't understand the way we talk?"

"Oh, there are many who can talk Russian."

"But why are we going there? Don't you like it here at grandma's?"

"I will tell you, but you must promise never to tell anyone."

"I promise."

"Word of honor?"

"Word of honor!"

"Papa is there."

"Papa! We are going to papa?"

"Yes. But you must remember you promised not to tell. No one, understand? If you tell, papa will have to go to war like uncle Misha. If someone asks you where papa is, say he is at the front."

"Which front?"

"The Caucasian front."

"There is no such front," I said.

"How do you know?"

"There are only 'language' fronts—like 'French', 'German', 'Turkish'."

(I was parading the knowledge I picked up from listening to continual conversations about the war.)

"Never mind what front. If anyone asks you, say papa is at the front. Remember, you promised not to tell. You gave your word of honor."

"I won't ever tell. Even if they stick me with bayonets, I won't tell."

"That's a good boy."

We went in March. I had gone on short train rides with grandpa on his business trips to neighboring towns. They lasted no more than an hour or two. But this one was to last two days and two nights. On long-distance trains in Russia all cars were equipped with berths. They were nothing like our Pullman berths, made up with sheets and pillows, although the first-class and possibly second-class carriages (called "soft" cars because the seats were upholstered) may have been equipped with them. In third class they were just wooden planks. Each compartment housed six people. During the day they sat three each on wooden benches facing each other. At night, two stretched out on these benches, two each climbed up to the upper shelves. They didn't undress. But this was fabulous luxury compared to our travelling during the civil war, following the revolution—in box cars or on open freight platforms.

Discomfort is nothing to a child. To me the trip was great fun. The train stopped at larger stations for half an hour or so. People went to the buffet for snacks or to fill their tea kettles with *kipiatok*. Hours were spent drinking tea and, of course, in conversing, the favorite Russian pastime. Some of the greatest scenes in Russian novels and short stories are set in railway carriages, where total strangers engage in serious conversation—about politics or their lives or their views on life or the fate of humankind.

When the train was stopped at a station, a single bong of a bell announced that it would depart soon. When the bell struck twice, the train would depart in a couple of minutes and it was time to get aboard. Three bongs were followed almost immediately by the conductor's shrill whistle, the engine's pro-longed "toot," followed by a short one and the jerky start. It was these ceremonies that made a long train trip an adventure in the eyes of a Russian child.

And here is something else that I will remember to the end of my days—a story mother told me as we left one of the stations. A rich lady traveling first class noticed from the open window an old bearded man in peasant dress on the platform. She called him over and said, "*Dyedushka* (granddad), would you please take this kettle and get it filled with *kipiatok* in the buffet?" "Sure, lady," said the old man and went on his errand. She waited nervously for him. He returned with the kettle just after the second bell. She thanked him and gave him a copper *piatak*. Then someone in the compartment asked the lady whether she recognized the old man. "No," she said, "why? Do you know him?" "That was Tolstoy," her travel companion told her.

Tolstoy was Russia's greatest writer, perhaps the most famous man in the world at that time. In his old age, he always wore peasant dress and traveled third class as a matter of principle because he always sided with the poor people (peasants and workers) against the nobles and the rich. The lady was terribly embarrassed. She rushed over to third class, found Tolstoy in a lively conversation with some peasants and asked him to return the tip she gave him. Tolstoy smiled good-naturedly and refused. "No, why should I give it up? I earned the *piatak* by honest work, perhaps the only money I ever made by real work." Tolstoy did not regard writing novels as "real work."

That was the first time I heard about Tolstoy. My real "acquaintance" with him, which was to become a major influence in my life, was to come two years later.

Toward the late afternoon of the second day the Caucasian mountains appeared far on the southern horizon. I had memorized the names of the highest peaks—Elbrus, Kazbek, Ararat. But the train was going over the flat plain of northern Caucasus. Except for those phantoms on the southern horizon, I never did see a mountain until we came to Crimea two years later.

We arrived in the morning after the second night. Father was there to meet us. It was a cloudy day, I remember, but quite warm. I don't remember how we got to where papa lived. It couldn't have been by *izvoshchik,* since I remember being carried. Possibly we went by *konka* and walked from the stop. I remember the address: 101 Bondarnaya Street. I saw Bondarnaya on a street sign. Father pointed at a gate across the street and said, "There is 90." I looked and saw a 90 (white numbers on blue background) and almost immediately I was looking at a lantern on our side of the street with "101" on its glass pane.

The place was a complex of one-story houses surrounding a central courtyard. Privies lined one side of that yard. There was no inside plumbing. Children played in the yard. Except for the stench from the outhouses, it was not a bad place to play. Water was delivered by huge horse-drawn vans and parked in the yard, while people came out with buckets to be filled. Peddlers kept coming throughout the day shouting their wares, sometimes in verse, sometimes in song.

This was the first time I played with kids aside from my cousins, Sonya and Volodya. When I was 3, before we moved to grandma's, mother sent me to a privately run kindergarten. But I don't remember playing with any of the kids. I was the youngest, and my precocity didn't help me much. All other children were older and they paid no attention to me except when I got hold of a toy that some other bigger child wanted. I remember, in particular, a rocking horse that I always wanted to ride. But I couldn't climb up on it. No kid would help me. Once the teacher helped me get on it. But as soon as she was gone, a bigger kid appropriated it. I was too intimidated to complain. In short, I wasn't happy in that kindergarten.

There was another reason I wasn't happy. Mother always prepared a lunch for me to take along—a sandwich and I don't remember what else, perhaps cocoa in a thermos bottle. All the children sat around the table with their lunches. I was a very slow eater, in fact, a poor eater. So all the others finished their lunches and left to resume playing, while I was still picking at mine alone at the table. And the teacher made me stay until I finished my lunch.

Once, when mother asked me how I liked going to the kindergarten, I told her about this situation. She took it seriously. The next day she made a lunch consisting only of an apple and a small sweet roll, saying that now I could finish ahead of everyone. I looked forward to it. On arriving I went straight to the teacher and to tell her that this time I won't have to stay at the table alone. She was busy with something and paid no attention. I persisted. Finally she turned angrily to me and said, "Now don't bother me. Go and play." When I reported this incident to mother, she pulled me out of that kindergarten. That was my first experience in trying to be a member of a group.

At 101 Bondarnaya I got another chance. There were many kids and all played noisily in groups. In particular there was one girl about 9 who reminded me strongly of Sonya. Sonya's fascinating trait was imagination. She would spin fantastic thrilling stories, some inspired by what she read, others of her own invention. It was she who later introduced me to world literature. The fantasy that particularly thrilled me was her prediction of what I would be when I reached her age. We shall live, she said, in a magnificent castle and will be fabulously rich. We shall be able to buy anything we wanted, because we would have quintillions of rubles. She even told me that we have already a few of these quintillions and showed them to me. They were clippings from magazines with pictures of some advertised products—fashionable clothes, bottles of wine, etc. Sonya said these pictures illustrate what can be bought with those quintillions. But at my suggestion to ask our parents to buy something with them, Sonya explained that these quintillions could not be used yet. We would have to wait until I was 9 years old, when we would move to our magic castle.

The girl who reminded me of Sonya always wore the same dress and went barefoot. This girl's family must have been poor. She took a liking to me and we spent time together, sometimes talking, sometimes just sitting quietly. Like Sonya, she had a vivid imagination. Once she told me she would take my picture. I was surprised. I knew what a camera was, having been photographed many times, and I couldn't believe that she had one. She told me to stand quietly and to put my hands behind my back. Then she pretended to snap a photo and went aside saying she was going to develop the picture. I watched her. She produced a hair pin and twisted it so that it formed the outline of a human body without arms ... just a loop, representing the head, the trunk—the twisted part—and the legs represented by the two ends of the pin. She said it was my picture. I asked about my arms. She said one couldn't see them, because they were behind my back. I was somewhat disappointed but I was impressed with her imagination.

As our friendship progressed, I told her about the magic castle that would materialize on my ninth birthday, about all the quintillions and the rest of it. I told her she would come to live with me and my cousin Sonya. I was astonished at her question. "And shall I have nice clothes to wear?" "Nice? You will be dressed in gold and silver like the czarina." She said nothing. It dawned on me that she didn't believe me. But I chased the bitter thought away.

That year the first *Seder* of Passover came on April 4 and we were invited by our hosts to participate. Uncle Mendel, the head of the family, told me that I would be allowed to taste some wine at that ceremony. He took out a dozen brass cups, spread them on the table and asked me which one I wanted to drink out of. They looked all the same, but I pointed to one, then wondered how uncle Mendel was going to recognize it. He nodded and put the cups away.

The previous year I had already participated in a Seder at grandpa's and even learned to ask the "Four Questions" in Yiddish, the privilege of the youngest boy at the table if he can do it. It went off very well. I especially remember the ceremony involving the prophet Elijah. At some point in the ceremony a tumbler of wine is filled to the brim and set in the middle of the table. The head of the family reads a prayer. Someone is sent to open all the doors. Then there is silence. Elijah (invisible, of course) is supposed to enter the house and take a small sip from the glass. In a few moments it was over. I tried to convince myself that the glass was now not quite full.

I don't know what we lived on. We may have had savings. Or else uncle Yevgeny may have helped us. We lived. Father crammed for the certificate of maturity. Of course he had no intention to enroll in a *gymnasia*. He planned to take the exam for all eight classes. Then he planned to enter some university.

There was hardly any greenery in Baku. The air was thick with the stench of petroleum from the refineries. There were two parks, however, that I remember. I think one was called Parapet, possibly because it was walled by a rampart on a steep hill overlooking the harbor. But I never saw that rampart. There was hardly any greenery in Parapet. At least I never saw any. I was sometimes taken to that park because it had a children's playground with swings and things. It was fashionable in those days to roll a hoop by hitting it with a stick. I was given a hoop like that on my fifth birthday in May.

The other park, again if I can trust my memory, was called Balkansky. That one was full of greenery, the only greenery I saw in Baku. Balkansky was where father studied. We went to it early in the morning, found a bench in the shade under a tree. Father read, made notes and sometimes asked himself questions aloud and answered them. And I listened. It was enough for me to be with father.

I remember being taken for a ride in a pleasure boat on the sea. I got seasick. I was told that on the shores of seas were beaches where people could go bathing in the saltwater. But there was no beach in Baku that I know of. I remember being with father near some warehouses on the coast of the Caspian Sea, where you could dive from a wooden platform. Some youngsters were there diving and apparently having a great time. Father, too, wanted to go in, but he didn't want to leave me alone, and I couldn't swim.

As mother had told me, the people in Baku were a mixed lot. The streets were teeming with traders. The trading usually consisted of intense bargaining, sellers shouting their wares, and so on. Advertising was mainly vocal. In short, Baku was a real Middle East city. I always thought it was like Baghdad must have been during the time of the caliphs and Arabian Nights. I was especially impressed with the *ambaly,* porters who carried some contrivance on their backs on which they put their loads. That was their occupation—lugging things. To this day, I don't understand why they didn't use wheelbarrows. For awhile I was afraid of them. I was told (possibly by my "girl friend" in our yard) that they kidnap children and carry them away on their backs. But I was skeptical and dismissed the idea.

Best of all was the opera. I was taken three times. The first opera I saw was Glinka's *A Life for the Czar.* The season always began with that opera. In Baku it opened in summer. So after the season was ended in Moscow and in St. Petersburg, the stars went to Baku. That is how I got to hear the greatest Russian opera singers, such as the tenor Smirnov, sometimes called the Russian Caruso.

I was most impressed by *A Life for the Czar.* My parents told me the story. The action is in 1613, the period that in Russian history was called "Time of Troubles." Poles invaded Russia, captured Moscow and put their own man on the throne. They were looking for the young czar, only a boy then, who was hiding out. To establish their own dynasty, they were going to do away with him. Ivan Susanin, a peasant, undertook to save the young czar. He pretended to guide the Polish detachment to his hiding place. Instead he led them into a swamp in the middle of the forest, from which they couldn't get out. When the Poles

56

found out that they were betrayed, they killed him. That's why the opera was called *A Life for the Czar*.

What I remember most vividly is the scene where a young boy (played by a woman) is knocking at the gate of a monastery and singing "Otvorite!" (Open!). I remember also the disappointment when the curtain went down and I didn't see the Poles killing Ivan Susanin. But my parents told me that was just the first act.

La Traviata was less impressive. The music was beautiful, but I didn't understand what was going on. I imagine my parents didn't explain to me the meaning of *demi monde*, as it applied to the heroine of the opera.

Rigoletto was something else again. There was the pathetic hunchback for whom I was sorry and the sinister Scarafucile with his threatening bass. And then there was the tune I knew well, "La donna e mobile" ("Beauties are fickle"), which my parents often hummed and which I heard played on a barrel organ, as the little monkey took coins from the "audience" (mostly kids) and doffed his little cap as he put the coins into the pocket of his little jacket. Imagine! It was part of an opera!

In fall, father passed his certificate of maturity exam and was preparing to apply to a university. Mother and I went back to Lozovaya. It was rainy and chilly. Unpaved streets were impassable. Vehicles would stick in the mud. People waited for winter snow, when wheels would be replaced by sledges. We were met at the station by uncle Borya and another young man. They carried our bags as we walked home. Uncle Borya said everyone was all right and that there would be a surprise for us at home. After all the embracing and kissing were over, we were taken to the parlor. And there was a grand piano!

MUSIC AND REVOLUTION:
A COTTAGE ON THE BANK OF THE VOLGA

The war goes on, and the news gets grimmer and grimmer.
Finally, revolution in 1917. For me it is a time of music.

GRANDPA'S BUSINESS IMPROVED DURING THE WAR. He was a middleman between the peasants and whatever agency stored grain. The millions in the army all had to be fed, while the number of men working the land was sharply reduced. So the price of wheat went way up, and grandpa had more money, not a windfall, just some money to spend on things that normally couldn't even be thought about. He bought a piano for uncle Borya, his younger son.

Borya played by ear. Alongside the house that grandpa built was his brother Meyer's house. They had an upright piano. Meyer's elder daughter Fenia played it. In fact, she was a professional who played piano in a movie theater. Of course movies were silent in those days, but it was oppressive to sit in complete silence while watching people "alive," as it were, talk to each other, rejoice when good things happened to them and suffer when misfortune struck. Now and then, the action was interrupted, and what they said was flashed on the screen instead of the picture. Sometimes an explanation of what was going on was flashed for a few seconds, just enough for an average reader to read it, so that the plot could be followed. But complete silence would have been unbearable. Later uncle Borya married Fanya, another cousin marriage within the Rapoport clan. Borya had a good ear. He was, to my knowledge, the only one in my extended family who was genuinely musical. And he was my first music teacher.

He taught me two pieces: the "Black Key Polka" and the "Revolutionary Funeral March." The polka sounded funny. The funeral march was a serious piece. I think it was composed to honor the victims of a massacre on January 9, 1905, the so-called Bloody Sunday. A large body of workers, mostly from the St. Petersburg steel mills organized a demonstration, a protest march along the Nevsky Prospect, the main thoroughfare of the capital leading to the czar's palace. They were led by a priest, Father Gapon, and carried icons. They meant to present a petition to the czar begging him to improve their hard lot—miserable wages, long hours, etc. Soldiers opened fire as the demonstration approached the palace. I don't know how many were killed, perhaps dozens, perhaps hundreds. The massacre didn't measure up to the massacre of protesting students in Beijing in 1989, but in those days it was considered monstrous. Bloody Sunday triggered the revolution of 1905.

Soon mother took me to a real music teacher. Her name was Anna Andreyevna Krupenia. She had studied in the famous Leipzig conservatory of music and at the time was a refugee from the war zone (I think her home was in Poland, which was part of the Russian empire then and occupied by the Germans).

Many such refugees were housed in Lozovaya, as well as prisoners of war.

I remember vividly my first meeting with Anna Andreyevna. She asked me to play what I had learned, and I produced the polka and the funeral march. Then Anna Andreyevna tested my ear. She would make me look away and played different keys on the piano, then would ask me to point to the keys she played. She said I had a good ear and would take me on as a pupil. She gave me my first lesson then and there.

From then on, I was taken to Anna Andreyevna for my lesson twice a week. The lessons proceeded following a rigid sequence of skill acquisition. I practiced monotonous scales and exercises, waiting impatiently to start playing "pieces."

It was the end of 1916, the last year of the czarist regime, the eve of the Russian revolution. The war was going on unabated. The Russians were losing. The Western Front, where the French and the British faced the Germans, was stalemated. The soldiers huddled in trenches behind barbed wire. Occasionally offensives were started by one side or the other, resulting in hundreds of thousands killed and wounded and no change in the situation. The survivors went back to their muddy, rat-infested trenches behind barbed wire.

About once a month a postcard came from uncle Misha, the prisoner of war in Austria, through the Red Cross. On the address side there were two questions to answer. One said "*Kuda?*" (Russian for "Where to?") The prisoner was to fill in the address. The other said "*Komu?*" (Russian for "To whom?") Here the name of the person addressed was to be filled in. On other side the message could be written in Russian. One of my aunts or uncle Borya would read it to grandma. From our side a package was sent once a month, largely cookies, which grandma baked.

Refugees from the war zones were sent into the interior and housed with private families. Also prisoners of war. For a while we had a couple with a baby housed with us. They were installed in the parlor. Later we had an Austrian prisoner of war. He was Jewish. (Jewish refugees and prisoners of war were housed with Jews.) German and Austrian Jews, unless they came from Galicia, generally spoke no Yiddish. But German (especially the Austrian dialect) is pretty close to Yiddish, so there was no difficulty of communicating with our "guest." Grandma was especially kind to him. She used to say that her kindness was sure to pay off: her son would be equally well treated in the Austrian prisoner of war camp.

As usual, I listened eagerly to the adults' conversations. Once I busied myself with building a contraption of wooden boxes and broom handles. I said it was a long-distance cannon. It would carry a missile to the "front," which wouldn't kill any one but would destroy all weapons, so the war would come to an end. There were always problems arising in the construction, so I never finished the job. The end of the war (for Russia) would indeed come soon, but not through my intervention.

One day uncle Borya rushed in waving a Moscow newspaper and shouting, "Franz Joseph is dead! Franz Joseph is dead!" I knew Franz Joseph was the emperor of Austria. So I asked if that meant that the war would soon end. The adults smiled. Some sighed.

But the next piece of news I heard was more exciting. Grandpa and I were both early risers and usually had our morning tea together. One morning, grandpa said to me. "The czar has changed places with his brother." I asked what that meant, but grandma intervened. "Don't talk politics to the child," she said in Yiddish, thinking I didn't understand. But I gathered this was something important, because the general mood changed.

The czar abdicated in early 1917. As usual, I found out what happened from conversations among adults. There was starvation in the capitals (St. Petersburg and Moscow). Again workers turned out to demonstrate, shouting, "Give us bread!" Soldiers were ordered to shoot at the crowds, but this time they didn't obey. The czar's throne was shaking. This was recognized by the highest functionaries of the government. The czar had replaced the commander-in-chief of the armed forces with disastrous results. He stayed at the army headquarters. A delegation of high officials was sent to him. They explained that Russia was on the brink of collapse, that the population no longer had any confidence in their czar. Nicholas II was not bright, but neither was he a ruthless despot, as his father (Alexander III) and his namesake (Nicholas I) had been (the massacre of January 9, 1905, notwithstanding). He agreed to give up the throne and named his brother Mikhail as his successor. But Mikhail said, in effect, "Thanks, but no, thanks." He understood that the monarchy was wrecked in Russia. So there was no more czar and no more government.

A provisional government was formed, led by Alexander Kerensky, member of the Socialist Revolutionary Party. It was understood that this government would rule until a Constituent Convention was formed of representatives elected by all adults of the Russian empire. There were no more official classes, just grazhdane (citizens). All restrictions imposed on Jews were abolished. Even women could vote. (In the United

States women couldn't vote until four years later.) The elected representatives would decide the political system of Russia, just as a convention of this sort established the United States in 1789. Many political parties, once underground, were legal since the revolution of 1905 and competed intensely in preparation for the Constituent Convention.

Then came the First of May. This was Labor Day (and still is) in all of Europe, but in czarist Russia it was forbidden to celebrate it. But now with the czar gone it was going to be an all-Russian wild party. Outdoor meetings were to be held everywhere with brass bands playing "La Marseillaise" (the French National Anthem) over and over again. It had been prohibited in czarist Russia because it celebrated the French revolution.

Then there were speeches and speeches and speeches. Everyone wanted to speak. And they had to shout to be heard. There were no microphones in those days. It didn't matter much, because practically everyone shouted the same slogans. Down with the old! Up with the new! Organize, comrades, organize!

On the First of May, when I got up, mother brought out my best shirt—a Russian shirt with a high button-up embroidered collar. It went over my pants down to my knees and featured a belt across the belly. She pinned a red ribbon on it and told me to go to have tea with the others. She told me to say to the family, "I am a Social Democrat—Bolshevik!" She explained that the main revolutionary parties were Social Democrat Bolsheviks, Social Democrats Mensheviks and Social Revolutionaries. They were all for equality of all citizens. She said we supported the Bolsheviks, because they were most determined to put an end to the war.

My declaration made quite a sensation. Then there was a lot

of heated discussion, which I didn't understand, but tried hard to pick up some words to use when the occasion arose. I especially liked the expression; "We must organize." I kept thinking how I could find out what it meant without disclosing my ignorance. The outdoor meeting was everything I looked forward to. Every one of the speechmakers sooner or later said, "We've got to organize!"

Father was not in Lozovaya then. He had passed his exams, got his certificate of maturity and was admitted to a university. It was actually the University of Warsaw. But it had been evacuated to Rostov-on-Don, because the Germans occupied all of Russian Poland.

Father was there finishing his first year in the faculty of law. He didn't come to Lozovaya till the term ended in June, I think. Through the rest of summer he was active in the organization of an elementary school for adults. Universal literacy was an issue on which practically all political parties agreed. Father taught reading, writing, arithmetic and geography. He also participated in politics. I went to several meetings where I heard him speak. Once I asked him how he thought up what to say in a speech. Father explained that there is no point in making a speech unless one has something to say. Then one simply says it. This idea seemed quite sensible to me. So I decided to make a speech.

I gathered a bunch of kids, I suppose about 15 or 20, telling them I would make a speech. I lined them up in two rows, told them to keep quiet and started talking. I said the adults keep saying that they've got to organize. So we kids have got to organize, too. I still had only a vague idea what it meant, but I knew that's what one had to say when one made a speech.

Then I told them what I really wanted to tell them: It was a shame that there were no apples. It used to be that someone always brought at least one apple from the market to give to a kid, and now there were none. I was carried away. I said if things went on like this we would grow thinner and thinner and become as thin as ...(here I tried to think of an apt comparison)... "as thin as threads!" I finally blurted out. That's the only thing I remember, and that, probably because it was talked about for a long time by adults who heard my speech.

It was a very happy summer, especially after father joined us. I continued my music lessons. On my birthday, May 22, I got a cheap briefcase to carry my music in, the most cherished of the presents.

It was then that I first was taken to the movies. Censorship was a thing of the past. So there was a movie about a revolutionary: *A Cottage on the Bank of Volga River*. It opened with a scene inside a railroad compartment. There were only two men in it, an arrested revolutionary and a gendarme guarding him. The gendarme gets sleepier and sleepier and finally nods and falls asleep. His captive stealthily opens the window and with great effort squeezes through it and jumps out. The scene shifts to the steep embankment, showing him rolling down and landing miraculously unhurt. He looks for a hiding place, sees a house in the distance on the bank of the Volga River, comes knocking on the door, explains his plight and asks the people to hide him. They turn out to be sympathizers of the revolution, and they take him in. That's all I remember. I'm sure there was some romance involved with the daughter of the house, but at my age I still did not appreciate these things. The most impressive thing was how the revolutionary escaped.

By a strange coincidence, 4½ years later father and I would also be hiding out in a house on a bluff overlooking a river, the border between Russia and Poland. Only it wasn't a neat cottage, but a miserable hovel. And our situation was not a movie, so there was no "love interest" involved.

After my sixth birthday, I was allowed to go about town alone within a prescribed area. Thus, I went to Anna Andreyevna alone, proudly carrying my briefcase. There was also a public library with a children's section. I got a card and was shown the shelves with children's books. They were numbered 1, 2, 3, etc. I took Number 1. It couldn't have been very interesting, since I don't remember what was in it. I returned it and took Number 2. It was even less interesting. I didn't finish it. Returning it, I asked the librarian whether it was permitted to take the next number without having finished the previous one. She laughed and explained that I didn't have to take the books in their order, that I could take any book on the children's shelves and that I could look it over to see whether it might interest me. This I did and soon found a book that was promising. It was about bees, their work, their adventures, their rallying to each other's assistance when one was in trouble and their noble slogan: "All for one, one for all!" It was then that reading became my favorite pastime. But all this ended abruptly when mother and I went down with typhoid fever.

The water in the well was evidently polluted. Everyone knew that you didn't drink unboiled water. But maybe there was a lapse and someone did. That's all it took.

I don't remember suffering much. I know mother did. She was delirious with high fever for several days. I remember only intense, chronic hunger. The standard treatment was starvation. For several weeks we had nothing to eat and only tea to drink. It was strongly sweetened, and the sugar kept us alive. My days consisted of waiting for that glass of tea to be brought in by grandma, who nursed us. I complained unless the glass was filled to the very brim. The high fever caused my skin to peel off. I helped the process by pulling big sheets of scorched skin off my arms. They looked like transparent paper. When the fever was gone after about seven weeks, we were allowed to get up. I had forgotten how to walk and had to learn all over again. Both of us had voracious appetites. I remember how delicious farina cooked in milk tasted, also soft boiled eggs mixed with chunks of toast. I used to hate soft boiled eggs. I grew fat. All of a sudden I lost my appetite and went back to skimpy eating. I became thin again.

This was in the end of summer 1917. In fall, father went back to the university in Rostov, and mother and I resumed our life without him. It was then that I made acquaintance with the works of Leo Tolstoy, which had a most profound influence on me for the rest of my life.

I DISCOVER TOLSTOY

*My Christianity dissipates through the years of the civil war,
but my affection for cousin Sonya grows, as does my admiration of Tolstoy's brilliance. I am spellbound by his literature.*

WINTER SET IN. THERE WAS LITTLE TO DO. Uncle Yania and his
family moved to Crimea, so I had no one to play with. I especially missed my mentor, Sonya. I practiced the piano, went to
Anna Andreyevna for lessons. I wanted very much to read, but
the folk tales lost their appeal. There was a colored comic sec-
tions of *Niva* ("The Cornfield"), a popular weekly, which our
neighbors subscribed to. But it had stopped publication, and
soon I read all the back issues of the comic section. I also had a
book given to me by father on my fifth birthday, all about the
daily life of a boy my age. But having read it through several
times, I was no longer interested in it.

My parents' library moved to grandpa's with us. I would
sometimes look into some volumes. I didn't understand what
they were about. I remember, in particular, a two-volume edition of Marx's *Das Kapital* in Russian translation, but it made

little sense. There was also a volume of Max Nordau, another translation from German. I got the idea that the two works were closely related, because Max sounded like Marx and both had the same binding—imitation marble.

Mother noticed my curiosity and told me I could read volumes 15 and 16 of Tolstoy's collected works. Leo Tolstoy was regarded as the greatest of the Russian authors, perhaps greatest in the world. The immense range of his writings included literature for children. There were many kinds of stories. I remember one about a boy who dreamt that he was given a bowl of his favorite porridge but had no spoon. So the next night, he took a spoon to bed with him. Unfortunately he didn't dream of porridge that night. Most of the stories contained some moral, or lesson. There was a story about a hen that laid golden eggs. The farmer who owned it thought there was a big piece of gold inside the hen. He wanted to get all that gold at once. So he killed the hen and opened it up. But all he found were giblets like those of any other hen.

Besides the stories there were simple lessons in geography, history and science. Geography was not at all like what my mother learned from standard textbooks—memorizing names of islands, rivers and peninsulas. Tolstoy's geography lessons were lively descriptions of other lands, their climates (some never had winter, some never had a real summer), the customs of other people. It was about how a desert or a jungle looked. History was not memorizing names and dates. There was a story of how a Cossack leader with a few hundred mounted warriors conquered most of Siberia. (That was before Tolstoy became a pacifist and renounced all war.) There were exciting stories about hunting. (That was before Tolstoy became a strict vegetarian and condemned killing any animal.)

I remember two lessons on general science. One was about how the sun is the source of practically everything we need in our lives. It not only gives us warmth directly, but its warmth is stored to be used when needed. For example, the standard fuel of the Russia peasant was lumber. Lumber comes from trees. Trees need sunlight to grow. So lumber is sort of "canned sunlight." We eat the flesh of animals. Cattle, sheep, goats feed on grass. Grass needs sunlight to grow. So when a man heats his house in winter or eats either bread or vegetables or meat, he is enjoying the gifts of the sun.

I remember a story about carbon dioxide. A woman is drawing water out of the well. The bucket drops off the hook and falls. The woman asks a neighbor to descend into the well to restore the bucket. He tells her that since she dropped it, she should go down herself but that he would help her get down there. So she sits on a stick tied to the rope, and he turns the wheel and so lowers her slowly down to the water level. All of a sudden he doesn't feel her weight. Looking down he sees her collapsed with her head in the water. He calls for help and asks to be lowered into the well. The same thing happens to him. Now there is a crowd around the well. One young man asks to be let down, and he ties himself to the rope. People watch as he goes down. Suddenly he lets go the rope and would have fallen in if he were not tied, so they pull him back up.

There is a teacher in that village who explains that there is no breathable air in the well at the water level. There is only carbon dioxide, which is useless for breathing. Being heavier than air, it always accumulates in low places.

I also remember a story about a traveler who stopped at an inn. While in bed, he discovered that the place was infested with bedbugs. Evidently they lived in the walls. So the traveler moved his bed to the middle of the room. It didn't help. Looking around, he found them making their way from the walls across the floor to his bed and climbing up the legs to get at him. He asked the innkeeper for four buckets, filled them with water and put a leg of the bed in each of them. Now he was sure the bed bugs wouldn't get at him. If they tried, they would fall into the buckets and drown. Congratulating himself on his cleverness, the traveler blew out the candle and climbed into bed. Soon he felt a bite. Bedbugs! How in the world did they get at him? Then he saw. They climbed up on the ceiling, then ran along the ceiling till they got over him, then dropped on him to continue their feast! I don't know whether this was a true story, but it certainly made an impression on me and got me thinking about intelligence in animals, about which we know so little. I was especially impressed by Tolstoy's assertion that a bedbug can smell a human being over hundreds of thousands of bedbug paces. I tried to figure out how far this was in human paces. The Romans called a thousand paces a mile. So hundreds of thousands of paces would be some hundreds of miles! At that time I didn't know anything about educational methods. But now I appreciate Tolstoy's deep insight into the secret of successful education of children: The first task is to capture and keep the kids' interest. He certainly captured and kept mine with these stories.

Volume 15 had arithmetic lessons, which I welcomed. There was information not contained in my *zadachnik,* for example Roman numerals. There were lessons on how to use the abacus, the primitive computing device universally used in Russia even as recently as the 1960s. On a visit to Russia at that time, I saw waiters in restaurants carrying these abacuses on their belts and expertly using them in adding up bills.

Volume 15 contained also *The Prisoner in the Caucasus,* the story set in Chechnya during its conquest by the Russians in the 1850s. A film was made in Russia based on that story and translated into our time, that is, the present bloody massacre in Chechnya. It was shown in a film festival in Toronto a few years ago.

But it was the stories in Volume 16 that impressed me most and made me revere Tolstoy for the rest of my life. During the last 20 years of his life, Tolstoy wrote practically no literature, such as novels. In fact, he as much as declared his masterpieces like *War and Peace* and *Anna Karenina* to be worthless. Instead, he wrote stories for the People (with a capital P) in the language of the People. Most of these stories were about lives of poor people, and they all carried a message, which, Tolstoy meant to be a lesson from the teachings of Jesus Christ.

Tolstoy regarded himself as a devout Christian. But actually he was excommunicated from the Russian Orthodox Church. In fact, it was prohibited to mention his name in public and his name could not appear in a newspaper. In the eyes of the government and of the church he became a non-person. Both the church and the government pretended that he didn't exist.

The reason he was excommunicated was that he refused to believe the dogmas of the Church. He denied the divinity of Christ. He denied that Jesus' mother, Mary, was a virgin. He said Jesus' father was unknown, and that is why Jesus called himself the "Son of God." He denied the doctrine of the Original Sin washed away by the crucifixion of Jesus. He said it was absurd to believe that God sent his only son to be killed (knowing that he would be killed) and that his blood would wash away the Sin (eating the forbidden fruit). He insisted that sacrifice of animals was sacrilege, let alone of a human being, let alone God's only son.

Tolstoy's simplified version of the Gospels addressed to children was in Volume 16. He insisted that the whole teaching of Jesus Christ amounted to just one truth and one commandment. The truth was that God is not some old man who lived in the sky but something that lived inside every human being. (We call it conscience.) And Tolstoy said there was only one commandment that contained the entire teaching of Jesus: One must love one's neighbor (that is, every other person including one's enemies) as oneself. According to Tolstoy this meant that one should not resist evil. One should return good for evil. Time and again he quoted from the Sermon on the Mount (a speech made by Jesus to an assembled crowd). If someone strikes you on your cheek, turn the other cheek, inviting him to strike that one too. If someone robs you of your coat, give him also your shirt.

It goes without saying that interpreting the teaching of Jesus, Tolstoy condemned all war without exception. To him there was no such thing as a "just war." He told people to refuse to serve in the army, because under no circumstances was it permissible to kill anyone for any reason whatsoever. Wherever peace can be made between people, it must be made. Whoever needs help should be helped. Helping another is the same as helping Jesus Christ. One of the stories in Volume 16 is just about that. It's the first story in Volume 16 that I read, and I've re-read it since many times.

Martin Avdeich, a poor shoemaker, lived in the basement of

a slum building. He was a widower left with a little boy, who was his pride and joy. And just as the boy became old enough to help Martin in his work, he fell sick and died. Martin became bitter and blamed God for his cruelty. Once a pilgrim stayed overnight with him. Martin complained to him about his misfortune. The pilgrim told him that he could find consolation in religion. Asked if he could read, Avdeich said he could. "Then read the Gospels," said the pilgrim. "You will find consolation there."

Avdeich followed the pilgrim's advice. The more he read the more he wanted to read. One evening, as he was absorbed in his reading, he fell asleep over the book, and suddenly he heard someone calling him: "Martin! Listen, Martin!" He mumbled in half sleep, "What is it? Who are you?" "Look out of the window tomorrow, I'll come to see you," said the voice.

The basement window was right by Martin's workbench. Out of it he could see only the feet of people passing by, but he recognized most of them. The people were from the neighborhood, and their shoes and boots often spent time in his basement workshop being repaired. So he recognized the people by their footwear. But when a strange pair of boots went by, he would bend down so that he could see the person. All the time he was expecting that "He" would come to see him.

Once he thought it was really "He," but it turned out to be only the janitor shoveling snow in front of his window. He felt foolish. "Must be getting feeble minded in my old age," thought Avdeich. "It's only Stepanich shoveling snow, and I thought it was Jesus coming to see me as He promised."

After a while he looked again. Stepanich was taking a break. It was clear that he was dead tired and freezing. Avdeich went up the stairs, opened the door and called to him, inviting him to come in. The old janitor came in. "Rest a bit and get warm. Want some tea?" The old man was most grateful. He drank three cups of tea and listened to Martin, who confessed to him that he was awaiting a visit from Jesus.

That was in the morning. At noon, he saw a young woman with a baby, who seemed to be in trouble. He invited also her to come in and get warm, shared his dinner with her and told her where she could get assistance. (She was left with the baby, as her husband was inducted in the army, and she came from the country to find a job but got lost, never having been in a city before.)

Dusk came, and still no Jesus. The last thing he saw was a woman beating an urchin. She had a basket of apples, which she was selling, and he tried to swipe one. Avdeich ran into the street and made her stop. He chided her for beating a defenseless child and finally made her ashamed. Then he gave an apple to the boy, promising to pay for it. He left the two walking together evidently having made friends. The woman had either forgotten or deliberately omitted to ask him to pay for the apple.

The day was over. Jesus never came. Martin lit his lamp and settled down to read. He was dead tired and fell asleep over the book. Suddenly in his sleep he heard someone calling him. "Martin!" He looked up and saw Stepanich, the old janitor in the dark corner.

"Don't you recognize me?" said Stepanich and smiled. "It's me." And he vanished.

Then the young mother with the baby appeared. "Don't you recognize me?" she said. "It's me." She smiled, and the baby laughed. And they were gone.

Finally the apple woman and the urchin appeared holding hands. "Don't you recognize me," each said. "It's me!" and both smiled and were gone.

Martin returned to his book and read the first sentence on the open page.

Inasmuch as ye have done it unto one of the least of these, my brethren, ye have done it unto me. (Matthew 25: 40).

I imagined that I became a Christian. I never mentioned Christianity explicitly. I felt this was not appropriate in grandpa's house. I did quote often from Tolstoy and said where I read it. I don't think grandpa or grandma ever suspected anything. Anyway, my "Christianity" dissipated during the years of the civil war.

I was much excited by the February revolution, I don't recall being impressed by the October revolution. I remember only the introduction of reformed spelling. Toward the end of winter, mother and I joined uncle Yania's family in Feodosia, and I was reunited with my younger cousin, now called Volodya by everyone but his father, who called him Izia (Isaac), and, what was most important to me, I was reunited with Sonya, now 12 years old. I continued as her most devoted disciple.

CHAPTER
9

FEODOSIA: FIRST SOJOURN

We move to Feodosia in the Crimea, later occupied by the Germans. I become part of a children's group ranging from toddlers to teenagers, (refugees from the north) and become absorbed in creative games and attempts at literature and drama.

UNCLE YANIA (SONYA'S FATHER) LEFT FOR CRIMEA while we were in Baku. I am not sure why or how he got around the residence restrictions that were in effect before the revolution. I suspect he moved there because he always wanted to be a farmer. There were no Jewish farmers in czarist Russia. Indeed Jews were not allowed to own land. However, the brothers of my maternal grandmother (the one who had emigrated to America) were all engaged in agriculture, not as farmers but as managers of large estates of mostly absentee land owners. Father always spoke of uncle Yania as a lover of the soil, rare among Russian Jews. He eventually did acquire a farm on the outskirts of Feodosia, the city to which we also moved. When we came, he did not yet have that coveted farm (that came later). He lived with his family in an apartment complex similar to the one in Baku, that is, a group of one-story, two- or three-room apartments around a central courtyard, in which children played. Unlike the kids in Baku, these kids became part of my life. If you recall, my only friend in the Baku complex was this girl, Sonya's age, whom I intended to make a princess in the magic castle (the one with the quintillions). In Feodosia, I became a member of a community of kids, ranging from 3-year-olds to teenagers.

In retrospect, I realize that they must have been middle class rather than slum kids like the ones in Baku. Their families all came from elsewhere. Perhaps they had fled the ravages of the Bolshevik revolution. Crimea was not yet sovietized. In fact shortly after we came it was occupied by Germans. Shortly after seizing power, the Bolsheviks made separate peace with Germany. Part of the peace treaty (canceled after Germany was defeated by the Allies) was separation of Ukraine from Russia. Ukraine became a puppet state of Germany and was occupied by German troops. I guess Crimea was regarded as part of Ukraine.

The kids in the complex were a sort of community. It was strictly stratified by ages. I recall there were two 3-year-olds, then a group of 5- to 8-year olds, to which my cousin Volodya and I belonged, then pre-teens, my 12-year-old cousin Sonya being the eldest, then a few teen-agers of both sexes. I think the eldest was a 15-year-old boy. The oldest kids acted as baby sitters for the youngest. Each group played games appropriate for their age. The older ones also organized "projects," in which the little ones also played parts.

One was to put on plays. Some even attempted to write them. Someone had a book entitled *Children's Theatre* or something like that. I was fascinated by some of the plays in it. I will describe some to give you an idea. There was one entitled *The Doll Revolution*. In the opening scene, a couple of rich, spoiled children are eating their lunch in the nursery. Their nanny serves them. They are rude to her and squabble among themselves. Their toys are scattered on the floor. Nanny tries to get the kids to put them away, but they pay no attention. Finally they all leave, and the toys come to life. The boys' toys are tin soldiers, a fierce hussar with a sword, a fireman, a clown. His sister's toys are dolls—babies, little girls, a brightly dressed peasant woman. The dolls are in bad shape. In a general conversation, they let the audience know how terrible life is with the spoiled brats. The delicate lady doll, a sort of forerunner of Barbie, complains that their constant yelling gives her a headache. Another doll points out that she doesn't even have a head—it has been torn off.

The hussar brandishes his sword and shouts that he will declare war on the brats. A general discussion follows. The clown proposes to change the children into dolls and themselves into children, then treat the brats as they treat their toys. These proposals and others like them are dismissed as impractical. Finally the female peasant doll proposes a sensible way out: "Let's just leave," she says, "we can go to the country and have some peasant kids adopt us. They'll appreciate us." All the toys agree enthusiastically. The scene ends with an exodus in marching order accompanied by music by the military trumpeter and the drummer.

The toys are adopted by peasant children, who treat their injuries (sew on torn limbs, provide the doll without a head with a head) and make them all happy. The rich kids finally track their toys down and come to claim them, but the toys refuse to go back. After much discussion and enlightening moralizing, peace is finally made and a compromise arrived at. The toys are divided between the rich and the poor kids.

I wasn't acquainted with children's literature in czarist Russia except for folk tales and that book. But there must have been more of the same. In fact, I have seen much Soviet children's literature. Sasha, my elder son, started out speaking Russian, and I read those stories to him. They all carried a moral message, like Aesop's fables.

Here is another play that I loved. *Little Red Flower* was the nickname of a young fabulously beautiful princess. The people worshipped her; she was a sort of forerunner of Princess Diana. As Little Red Flower rode through the city in her carriage, the people bowed to her, praising her dazzling beauty. One day she came back from the ride weeping. An old man in the crowd refused to bow to her. Instead, he shouted, "I won't bow down to you; you are not worthy!" Little Red Flower's nanny explains that people honor not only beauty but also learning. So Little Red Flower decides to become learned. A procession of scholars enters: the astronomer wearing a tall star-spangled hat and carrying a telescope, the mathematician with a multiplication table and a compass, the biologist with stuffed animals, the philosopher with a stack of books and a stuffed owl (the symbol of wisdom). Each tells Little Red Flower what he is going to teach her. It's clearly for the benefit of children in the audience. All good theater and good advertising. The curtain falls. When it rises, a few minutes later, Little Red Flower has become learned, and every one knows it now. But again she comes back from her ride bitterly disappointed. The old man refused to bow to her again shouting, "You are unworthy!"

You can surmise what happens next. There is a famine in the land and Little Red Flower insists that the granaries be opened up to the starving people. This time the old man bows deeply as the princess rides by and shouts, "I honor you for your great heart!"

I hoped one of those exciting plays would be adopted for our performance, but the big kids vetoed my proposals. They chose the shortest and simplest, a one-act play, entitled *The Christmas Tree*. I was given a single line of only four words, something about how grand the tree looked.

The kids also tried to write plays. But that didn't pan out very well. I remember only one that was performed in the yard without stage or props but with elaborate make-up and costumes. It was written and produced by a 10-year-old of Greek descent, who also played one of the four characters.

The cast: A young lover (played by the author); his beloved, whose rich parents disapprove of the poor suitor; and the parents. Much work went into making the adults credible. The mother was corseted, heavily powdered and rouged, wore a grotesque coiffure. The father was mustachioed, wore a pincenez and a cutaway morning coat. The lover wore his ordinary clothes. Get it? For contrast.

Act one. The young lover pretends to knock on the girl's bedroom. "Who's there?" "It's me. I have come to take you away." And so on. The girl is frightened. hesitates, but finally relents and they leave.

Act two. The parents are sad. They have a lonely old age to look forward to. "Let us forgive them," says the mother. The father agrees. "But we don't know where they live," says the mother. "I do," says the father. "An old partner of mine lives in

Athens, and he met them there. They are married now." "Oh, let us go there at once," says the mother, and they start packing.

Act three. The young people in their apartment in Athens. He: "Very interesting news in the paper today. Too bad you can't read Greek." She: "I have a surprise for you. I have learned Greek in secret. And I have read the paper." She begins to tell the news she read. Her husband is delighted. They embrace. A knock on the door. It's the parents. Touching reunion. Tears and kisses. Curtain. I didn't think much of the play.

For a while I toyed with the idea of writing a play but gave it up. I didn't think the big kids would take the trouble to produce the play I had in mind with all the staging and props that it required, and I didn't want a "make believe" production. I can't remember it now except that it had something to do with the revolution. It was pretty elaborate with crowd scenes and so on, and there weren't enough kids to make a crowd.

Once the kids undertook to publish a magazine of original stories, articles and news items about events in the complex. Everything was hand-written; about a dozen issues were produced, which were loaned to the adults, who were asked to circulate them around. On another occasion a "war" was staged between the boys and the girls, in which physical violence was strictly forbidden and casualties were acted out symbolically according to strict and elaborate rules. Since I firmly refused to regard my cousin Sonya as an enemy, I was allowed to join the girls' side. Naturally I was mercilessly teased, but I gloried in my martyrdom.

In the spring of 1918 the Germans occupied Crimea. Immediately after seizing power, the Bolsheviks arranged for a separate peace with Germany. The terms amounted to the dismantling of the Russian empire. German troops occupied the Ukraine, that is, practically all of southern European Russia, including Crimea.

In the middle of our apartment complex was a *besedka,* some benches in a circle around a table with a roof over them but no walls. Neighbors could sit and talk in this *besedka* on warm summer evenings and drink tea from a *samovar.* The Germans requisitioned

Author's father in uniform of a university student

the *besedka* and quartered five or six soldiers in it. They slept on the benches and cooked their food on kerosene burners.

At first, we kids were afraid of them. My cousin Sonya did not always distinguish her fantasies from reality and told me the Germans had hand grenades. Once she got hold of a carpenter's plumb line—a conical weight on a string—and told me that it was a hand grenade. By and by we got used to the Germans, and they were nice to us.

In the fall of 1918, Father was a second-year university student in Rostov-on-Don. When the Germans left Crimea, we went back to Lozovaya.

10

SEE, NO GUN.
NOW, THEN, WHERE'S THE MONEY?

Lozovaya is a hub of the civil war. The Reds, the Whites, the Ukrainian nationalists and assorted bandit gangs come and go. Every group is an enemy of every other. The inhabitants are abused and terrorized in varying degrees by most of the warring factions. Only the Reds turn out to be comparatively decent.

SHORTLY AFTER THE BOLSHEVIK REVOLUTION, the czarist army broke apart. The soldiers simply left the front and went back to their villages. There was no one to stop them. If some officers tried, the soldiers killed them. The officers were practically all from the upper classes and some were willing to fight the Bolsheviks. Their goals differed. Some wanted to restore the monarchy, others favored the establishment of a democratic republic. But they were all united by a common hatred of the Reds. Some high-ranking generals organized these anti-Soviet officers into armies.

A czarist general Krasnov formed an army of Don Cossacks to fight the Bolsheviks. He made Rostov-on-Don his headquarters and declared a universal draft, in particular of university students. Father fled. We were told that he went to Lozovaya. The Germans, defeated by the allies, had left. Lozovaya was temporarily a no man's land. Father was elected mayor and organized a self-defense unit composed of young Jews armed with anything that could be found—swords, axes, hunting shotguns. They patrolled the town on horseback, quite a feat for men who had never ridden a horse. However, when Ukrainian nationalists occupied the town, father, as a leader of an armed Jewish group, was a prime target. He escaped again. No one could tell us where he went.

Later we heard that father was in Feodosia. Having found out that we were in Lozovaya, he tried to come to join us, but it was at that time impossible. Crimea was occupied by some other warring faction, and there was no communication between it and the Ukraine. Life in Lozovaya during the winter of 1918-19 was precarious.

The political situation changed as capriciously as the weather. Sometimes the Reds were in power, sometimes the "Haidamaki," as the Ukrainian nationalists called themselves, sometimes totally unpredictable partisans.

Life was relatively secure under the Reds. At any rate, the Red Army troops were most disciplined, didn't pillage and didn't single out the Jews to pick on. They even tried to establish a semblance of normal life. I remember a concert by local talent, in which I participated. Some sang, some presented humorous skits. Recitation of poems was always very popular in Russia. A 12-year-old pal of mine, regarded as a roughneck disliked by parents, recited a fiery heroic poem, like "The Boy Stood on the Burning Deck" or "The Face on the Bar Room Floor," the kind that used to be recited at grammar school commencement exercises in America. When I graduated from elementary school in Chicago in 1923, I recited the Gettysburg Address. They assigned it to me to show how successfully they Americanized immigrant children.

The mayor, a Communist functionary, also recited a poem with a political message. There was complete silence when he made his bow. The Lozovayans welcomed the Red Army as a relief from the Haidamaki and the roving partisan bands, but they had no love for Soviet power and its draconian measures designed to destroy their accustomed way of life.

My uncle Misha had returned from the Austrian prisoner-of-war camp. He had a very decent baritone voice. In fact, he was an important figure in Austria organizing "concerts" by prisoners of war, in which he also participated. So naturally he was invited to sing a number at the concert in Lozovaya. He was impressed by my accomplishments on the piano and insisted that I, too, play a number. So I played a piece entitled "The Wounded Eagle." I could play it by heart, but uncle Misha insisted that I play it from music to show that I could read music. He sat beside me and turned pages. He was pleased to learn that some people in the audience assumed that he was my teacher.

The interlude under the Soviets didn't last long. Under onslaughts by one or another of the warlords, the Reds retreated to the north. Lozovaya became no-man's-land. This time there was no one to organize a committee of self-defense, and the Jews became the number one prey of the marauding bands.

It seems some bandits developed a technique of looting with a minimum of violence. Coming into a house they would announce politely that they were now the authorities in the town and that in order to ensure law and order, they must make sure there were no weapons in private hands. Then they proceeded to search the house. If they saw something they liked (and they liked many things) they would ask whether their hosts would like to contribute it to their cause, which was usually described as the people's struggle for a free and democratic Ukraine.

On one occasion, I remember they saw some red cloth they liked. Our "visitors" were Petlura's Haidamaki, at the time the Bolsheviks' strongest enemies in the Ukraine. They were distinguished by red hoods pinned behind their caps. That's what they wanted the red cloth for. Naturally, we couldn't very well refuse.

As I recall, we had five such visits. The last one, with shooting, was the scariest. But the one I remember most vividly was one that I named in retrospect "See? No gun! Now then ..." I don't remember which band that was. They came in without the usual explanation, "We're searching for privately held weapons." Uncle Misha received them. Putting it mildly, grandpa was not a brave man. When characters like these came, he usually went to bed, and the guests were told that the head of the household was sick. So uncle Misha received them.

This time it was early in the morning, and uncle Misha had been shaving. He came out with his face all lathered without a shirt, suspenders hanging behind him. It was a good thing he didn't come out absentmindedly holding his razor, which might have been misinterpreted with fatal consequences. The leader pointed a *nagan* at uncle Misha's belly and demanded, "Where's the money?"

Uncle Misha was stricken dumb with fear. He tried to say something, but only weak stuttering came out. His sister, my aunt Rose, was the only one in the family who kept her cool when the bandits came.

"Dobrodiu," she said (meaning "sir" or, sometimes "benefactor" in Ukrainian), "can't you see? The man is so scared he can't talk when a gun is pointed at him. Put your gun away, then tell him what you want."

"You're right, girlie," said the thug. He nodded to aunt Rose, then put the gun behind his back and wiggled the fingers of his left hand before uncle Misha's nose. "See, no gun," he said, "Now, then, where's the money?"

I was having my morning tea when they came, so I saw the scene. I don't recall much more of that incident. Evidently it came off without bloodshed.

But that wasn't the worst of the "visits." The worst was probably by members of the Machno gang, the most ferocious of the Ukrainian guerilla bands. It was during a brief period when Lozovaya was apparently no man's land with no authorities to keep a semblance of order. In the evening, my aunt Tsina went out on some errands. We had an arrangement about coming back from errands—to ring the bell shortly once or, perhaps, twice by way of a password.

We heard the bell ring. But it was not the password ring. It was wild prolonged ringing. The bandits came on to the porch, just as aunt Tsina was about to ring the bell and ordered her to answer that it was she when asked, "Who's there?" She deliberately rang wildly to warn us that something was not right. Aunt Rose went to open the door. The first thing we heard was a pistol shot. It went wild. Aunt Rose ran screaming. Everyone scattered as the bandits broke into the living room shooting wildly. My aunt Pasha (mother's youngest sister, who was then about

18) fainted and couldn't be revived until long after the bandits left.

It was evening. I was eating buckwheat kasha with milk out of a cup. Mother grabbed me and took me in her arms. I grabbed the cup. We ran into the apartment where we lived. There was a closet off the kitchen. It could be locked from the outside but not from the inside. Someone of the household ran past the closet. Mother opened the door and asked him or her to lock us in. So there we sat in the darkness. I was scared. I grabbed mother around her neck, and we sat there afraid to make a sound. We heard screams and shooting. We thought everyone was massacred.

I don't know how long we stayed like that. Nor do I remember much of what happened afterwards. What I will be telling now is my mother's recollections. After some time of ominous silence, mother heard someone calling "Adel Pavlovna! Adel Pavlovna!"

Adel Pavlovna is mother's Russian name and patronymic. Adult acquaintances not intimate enough to call each other by first names call each other by name and patronymic.

For example, I am called Anatoli Borisovich (since Boris is my father's Russian name). Grandpa's Hebrew name was Pinchus and somehow this was russified to Pavel. So mother was Adel Pavlovna.

The fact that someone was calling for "Adel Pavlovna" was most significant. Surely no one in the family would call her that. And most surely not one of the bandits. So who could it be calling "Adel Pavlovna?" There were guests in the house when the bandits broke in; so it may have been one of them. Or maybe it was some people who answered the desperate screams "Help! Help!" that we heard when the bandits were in the house. Anyway the bandits must have gone, so it was safe to start shouting to be let out of the closet. And sure enough, someone came, unlocked the door, and we emerged blinking in the light.

Except for aunt Pasha, who was still in a swoon, no one was hurt. Evidently the bandits panicked. It was someone else's house that they intended to terrorize and raid. So they lost their way and desperately tried to get out. They grabbed one of the guests and shouted to show them the exit, which he willingly did, and they were gone. Other people from the neighborhood came in, and everyone was accounted for, except my mother and me. That's why someone started calling "Adel Pavlovna!" which mother interpreted as "all clear."

That was the last of the raids. Soon the Reds came back, and again life became almost normal. The family could even celebrate Passover. Of course there was no way to buy matzoth, so we made it ourselves. The whole family was mobilized. Dough was rolled into thin sheets. The holes in these sheets were made by a little cogged wheel run back and forth on the dough. The cogs made the holes. That, incidentally, was my job, which I did with gusto. At the Seder I put a cap on without being told, which pleased grandpa very much, and I asked the traditional Four Questions, and the prophet Elijah came and took a sip of the wine. And the traditional trick was played on grandpa: stealing the last piece of matzoth from under the pillow on which the head of the household traditionally sat at the Seder. And then the ransom for it is demanded.

That was a happy time that spring of 1919. The best part of it was that the territory from Lozovaya to the Crimea was now all under Soviet control. That meant that we were able to go to Feodosia and join father, from whom we were cut off all winter.

There were practically no money transactions in the first years of Soviet rule. Certainly not in transportation. Freight trains ran occasionally with empty boxcars. If you could manage to get on one, you traveled. After some waiting, we managed to catch one going south, and we got aboard. No questions asked. A number of Red Army men were traveling in the same boxcar. Some took a fancy to me, asked me where mother and I were going. I told them that my father was in Feodosia and that mother and I were cut off from him in Lozovaya until the Reds came, and that now were going to Feodosia to join him. And one of them asked me whether I was glad that the Bolsheviks were winning the war against the Whites, who, he said, wanted to bring the czar back, and asked how my father felt about this. And I told them that all of us were on their side, that only the Reds were decent to us in Lozovaya, and we got talking about politics.

This same Red Army man started telling me about what life would be like when Soviet power is established in all Russia. He said there would be neither rich nor poor, that everything was to be divided equally, and everyone would have enough of everything. There was another Red Army man who wasn't so nice. He kidded me about my "class origin" and about grandpa, who, as I told him, was in some sort of business. He said when under Soviet power all the "bourgeois," which, he explained were neither workers nor peasants and lived by other people's labor, would be treated as they deserved. And he even went on with some cruel teasing. He said there would be a limit to how long people were allowed to live, because old people stop working and are of no use to the working people. He said 55 would be the age limit for everyone, then went on to ask me how old my grandpa was. But the other nice Red Army man cut him off and told me to pay no attention to him.

I think the journey lasted at least 24 hours. (The distance from Lozovaya to Feodosia is about 280 miles.)

CHAPTER

11

FEODOSIA: THE LAST SOJOURN

Uncle Yania buys a farm, father becomes a businessman and I go to plays and concerts, become a voracious reader and practice my English. Feodosia becomes a cultural center fed by the stream of refugees. Finally the Reds occupy Crimea and "punish" it for being the last stronghold of the Whites. Whatever food supplies are left are sent north and starvation sets in. Whites who couldn't escape are machine-gunned in mass executions.

WHEN WE CAME, CRIMEA WAS HELD BY THE REDS. This is what made our coming there possible, and we were again reunited with father, this time never to part again. But a short time afterward, the Whites took over, possibly the forces of general Denikin, who was the most successful of the anti-Soviet warlords. He organized his army in the northern Caucasus and carried on an offensive that carried his forces in the fall of 1919 to within striking distance of Moscow. But he was thrown back and his army disintegrated. Wrangel, the last of the White warlords, was now bottled up in Crimea, the last stronghold of the counterrevolution.

Wrangel was able to hold out because Russia's erstwhile allies—England, France, Italy and Romania—all supported him. They still hoped to put an end to the Soviet regime. So their warships were constantly seen in Crimean harbors, of which Feodosia was one. Both England and France (the Entente, as the Bolsheviks called them) were most generous with their aid, which spilled over to the civilian population. Feodosia became a boom town. Business flourished. It also became a refuge for the well-to-do fleeing the Soviets and a cultural center, since among the refugees were stars of drama, ballet and music.

We came back to the apartment complex in which we lived previously, but only for a short time. Soon we moved nearer the center of town into a large room, part of which served as living room and bedroom and part as kitchen. The address was 1 Italian Street. Next to it was an empty lot on which I practiced my English. The harbor was within walking distance.

My uncle Yania finally realized his life's dream. He bought a farm just outside the city; raised fruits, vegetables and poultry. Father became a businessman. He always hated the idea but somehow a living had to be made in a business environment. He went into partnership with another man, and they opened a leather store. Ready-made clothes and footwear were still rarities in Russia. Clothes and shoes were made by tailors and cobblers. Leather for boots and shoes was sold in the story that father and his partner bought.

They did very well. Business was brisk. For the first time in their lives my parents were well-to-do. We ate well, dressed well. Winters were mild in Crimea, but I became possessor of a *podiovka,* a national Russian overcoat with fur trimming.

We went to concerts and plays. Anna Andreyevna, my first music teacher, also came to Feodosia. My lessons resumed, and we bought a grand piano. I also had private lessons in French and English. I did not do well in French, didn't like the teacher much. But I liked the young woman who taught me English, and I made progress.

I practiced my English on an empty lot next to the apartment complex where we lived. That's where British sailors played soccer. Several kids gathered to watch. When a ball went wild, they all rushed to get it, competing to bring it to a sailor, who often smiled at them and said something in English. It was a thrill. The kids worshipped the British.

There was no central courtyard in the apartment complex on Italian Street. I missed the "children's republic." My friends were now all boys about my age (8–10), who lived nearby. We met on the street, played in the empty lot when the sailors didn't play soccer or else walked up and down the street talking and arguing, mostly about war. Tolstoy the devout Christian was forgotten. War was all around us.

Wrangel's army consisted predominantly of officers. They were in natty uniforms (financed by the Entente) and were everywhere in the stores shopping, in audiences at performances, riding in horse-drawn carriages. Glamour. Warships constantly came and went. The boys learned to recognize the types: destroyers, cruisers and so on. Dreadnoughts were mentioned with awe (they were equipped with 16-inch guns), but I don't remember seeing any. There were lively arguments about who were the best warriors—the British or the French. Practically all boys rooted for the British. Some backed their arguments by reference to James Fenimore Cooper's romantic novel about the French and Indian War, *The Last of the Mohicans*. Not to be outdone, I rooted for the French citing from Schiller's *The Maid of Orleans,* which I had read in Zhukovsky's translation.

My playmates were all middle class. And by middle class one understood the educated. Yes, Russian, especially Russian-Jewish children read a lot even before adolescence. Boys, to be sure, read mainly, perhaps even exclusively adventure literature, practically all translations, since there was no Russian adventure literature to speak of. That's why we talked about war: that "adventure" was always around us.

Practically all the boys I met were from families who fled the Reds. So they all rooted for the Whites. And some of this bias rubbed off on me. There were propaganda cartoons plastered all over town. I was especially impressed by one, which depicted Moscow with its onion-shaped church domes enveloped by an immense dragon labeled Bolshevism. Rushing at the dragon was a rider wielding a giant sword. He represented Wrangel's army. My admiration of the Whites and the Entente navy didn't last long. My cousin Sonya, who was my ultimate mentor, said that when the Whites see the peaks of Red Army helmets rising about the horizon, they will rush to the ships of their allies and flee to Turkey, at least as many of them as can squeeze in. And this is the way it came about.

Anyway, the fascination with war didn't last long. Russia's theatrical aristocracy fleeing the Reds (musicians, actors, dancers) was bottled up in the Crimea. My parents started taking me to concerts and to plays, and I became completely absorbed with them. One concert featured Smirnov, Russia's leading tenor, Kaidanov, a baritone, and a pianist, who accompanied both and played his own composition entitled "Faust." The audience went wild over Smirnov, kept calling for encores, some shouting "Lensky's aria!" (from Tchaikovsky's *Eugene Onegin),* some for "La donna e mobile" from *Rigoletto.* I rooted for the latter, recalling the opera in Baku, but Smirnov sang neither. He chose some romance, called "Tishina" ("All Quiet"). Brought the house down. The baritone sang Mephisto's aria from Boito's *Mephistopheles,* which I was to hear in Chicago just three years later. The pianist's composition was weird, but I was much impressed by his wild gestures as he played. I tried to imitate him at home, but mother told me to stop it.

Of the plays I recall one was Schiller's *Robbers* and one called *Satan,* whose author I don't remember. The latter was another version of the recurring theme of Satan's struggle with God. As in Goethe's *Faust,* the prologue is an ongoing argument between the two. As usual, Satan maintains that he can corrupt any human being. He had failed to corrupt Job, the God-fearing stoic of the Old Testament, and he failed to corrupt Faust, the seeker of knowledge and ecstatic experience. But now he undertakes to corrupt the most pious Jew. So he takes on human shape and becomes the pious Jew's partner in business. He urges the righteous one to buy a lottery ticket. At first the latter has misgivings. If he wins all that money, he argues, won't some lose it? Satan assures him that this will not happen. So the pious Jew wins a fortune, and that starts his corruption. Nevertheless he eventually sees the light, and Satan loses his bet again.

One day father didn't come home from the store, and a neighbor of ours, a young seamstress told us he was arrested. We were desperate. Mother had no idea what to do. But he came home the next day and told us about it. I could never imagine father having any enemies, but evidently in the business world anything can happen. Perhaps someone informed the authorities that father had communication with political prisoners, that is, with jailed suspected communists or communist sympathizers. The investigator turned out to be intelligent and decent. Father readily admitted that he was a socialist, but explained that, as things turned out, socialists could not possibly collaborate with communists, since the Bolsheviks persecuted socialists more energetically than any of their enemies, real or presumed.

Father got off, but the worst was yet to come. One morning mother answered a knock on the door and a formidable colonel came in. Omitting any explanation he demanded, "Where is my laundry?" Mother could barely stutter, "Wh...at laundry?" The colonel blew up. "You know very well what laundry. Now get this: if my laundry is not here by 2 o'clock, a shake-up will start in this place and will spread over the whole city. *You people* know what to expect!"

Indeed we knew whom he meant by "you people," and we knew what to expect, once things got started. During the war in the Ukraine, my grandmother's two brothers were killed in a pogrom. Another White Guard officer, I think a lieutenant, lived in our complex with his old mother. In despair mother appealed to him. He said he would go to headquarters and see what could be done. When he came back he reported that the situation was very tense and that all he could do was declare that he was not involved in this affair, thus shielding himself and his mother from any unpleasantness. It was now noon. In despair, mother told the young seamstress what threatened. She was Jewish too. But she said brightly,

"Oh, I know what must have happened. Yesterday a soldier, probably the colonel's orderly, brought me some shirts to be repaired. They must have been the colonel's. And he had another bundle with him, which must have been the laundry. I told him I did not wash laundry and directed him to a woman who does. I know where she lives."

By 2 o'clock, the laundry was in place, the orderly came to pick it up, and the pogrom was forestalled.

Months later, when the Reds were already in Feodosia, father met the colonel in the yard, now in civilian dress, evidently hoping not to be spotted as a White Guard officer. Like father, he was chopping wood for the stove. He approached father and said, "I assume you are going to report me. Perhaps I can make it worth your while not to do so. I have no money, but I have a number of items that may interest you."

Father assured him that he had no intention of reporting him. They met in the yard several times after that and exchanged "Good morning." Later he disappeared. So did the young officer, who made sure that he and his old mother were not mistaken for Jews during the pogrom.

During those two years in Crimea I became a voracious reader, mostly under Sonya's tutelage. She introduced me to the rich foreign literature read primarily by children and adolescents, which had no parallel in Russia. I read the Grimm brothers, Hans Christian Andersen, Selma Lagerlof, Mark Twain, R.L. Stevenson. I was introduced to science fiction, at first of Jules Verne, then of H.G. Wells (*The Invisible Man*), finally to adult literature—Dickens (*Little Dorrit, Oliver Twist, Domby and Son*), Gogol (*Evening on a Farm Near Dikanka*), Pushkin (*The Captain's Daughter*). Sonya would summarize the plots before giving me these books to read, and sometimes let her imagination run away with her to make the plots more dramatic. Inadvertently, much of the Russian classics remained unread. With this treasury I became acquainted during my first years in America.

Crimea was under siege through the fall of 1920. The Reds stormed the fortress Perekop on the isthmus connecting Crimea to the mainland and invaded the peninsula. The allied warships left, and the Whites scrambled for places on whatever sailed to Turkey. Thousands were left to the mercy of the victors.

Early one morning we saw the Red cavalry riding leisurely past our windows on Italian Street. Later that day there was a knock on our door and five Red Army men appeared. They told us politely that they were billeted with us and stayed. Father bid them welcome. They brought their own blankets and slept on the floor. They also had their own rations, which they often shared generously with us. There was, of course, no business of any kind, no open stores, no markets. A rationing system was introduced.

The unit stationed in Feodosia was the Thirtieth Siberian Division, famous for its discipline. Their treatment of the civilian population left nothing to be desired. Our guests were Kazan Tartars—jolly, good-natured fellows. One of them played Tartar folk tunes on the piano, using only the black keys, because they form the pentatonic (five-tone) scale on which that folk music is based. After a week or so they left. The Ninth Division, which replaced the Thirtieth, was quite different. Their rule began with an order for all former members of the White Army to register. The stranded ex-Whites hesitated, fearing the worst. Some, however, registered and were not detained. The others then became encouraged and registered.

Next they were asked under some pretext to register again. This time all went reassured that there was no danger. But now they were all detained and imprisoned. A few weeks later they were taken out of town at night and machine-gunned. The executions took place within shouting distance of uncle Yania's farm. The family heard the screams of the victims. We assume that is what happened to the colonel who fumed about his laundry and to the lieutenant who saw to it that he and his mother would not be taken for Jews in case of a pogrom over the colonel's missing laundry.

The city settled down to a dreary, hungry existence. There was no trade of any kind, thus no food to buy. People subsisted on rations. Father went to work for the Department of Education. His pay was a pound and a quarter of black bread per day: a half pound for him (a worker), a half pound for me (a child), a quarter pound for mother. Mother had secreted a few pounds of barley. That supplemented our diet for a while. Occasionally handouts were distributed. I remember two: on one occasion three eggs, on another a slab of mutton. Whenever anything was found on the shelves of the deserted stores, it was fairly distributed. On one occasion we got a can of shoe polish, on another a jar of jam of some kind. I came down with pneumonia and barely made it. Actually Crimea was being punished for having been a haven to the White warlord. So all food was shipped north. Father recalls boxcars with signs on the doors: A GIFT TO RED MOSCOW FROM RED CRIMEA.

In April 1921, father was given a month's leave of absence with a voucher to travel to Lozovaya. In the Ukraine the New Economic Policy, under which trade was permitted, was in full swing and food was plentiful. One car of a freight train was equipped as living quarters with sleeping platforms and a stove to cook on (it was known that the trip would take several days).

We (three families of us) boarded that boxcar on a bright April day and in less than 24 hours we were on the way.

CHAPTER

12

LOZOVAYA: POINT OF NO RETURN

Another trip from Crimea to Lozovaya means nine days in a boxcar. This time there is no turning back. My parents reach a difficult decision. We will leave Russia.

BEFORE RAILWAYS WERE BUILT IN RUSSIA, people traveled cross-country by horses. The well-to-do had their own carriages, but they couldn't use their own horses for long journeys because the horses had to rest longer than the people. So the horses were provided by the government. There were stations spaced far enough apart to allow covering some 30 or 40 miles at a stretch. So one went into the inn for a meal and a rest. The horses were left at the station, a new team hitched on to the carriage, and the journey continued.

The journey was full of drama. You never knew whether horses would be available at the next station. It depended on whether horses were on hand and on the rank of those waiting. There was no such thing as first come first served.

We traveled from Feodosia to Lozovaya by rail, but it was the same as traveling by horse. For some reason, during the civil war in Russia the engine had to be changed at every large station. I don't know why. I didn't think that an engine would get tired and would have to rest. Maybe repairs were always needed even after a short trip by those ancient engines. Anyway that's the way it was. We would travel to the next major station. The engine would be unhitched, and we would have to wait until a fresh one was available. That's why the 280-mile trip took nine days. We could do nothing about it. I hated these stopovers. I was painfully impatient to see grandpa and grandma and my aunts and uncles.

Sometimes at night I felt the train moving and was overjoyed, thinking we were on the way again. But it always turned out that we were being switched from one track to another. Someone in our car quipped, "These are free rides they are giving us."

Peasants came to meet the train with bread, potatoes, chickens and slabs of bacon.

Outside of Crimea the NEP was already in force, and things could be bought for money. Father was supplied with some Soviet money when he was given his leave of absence.

Life seemed almost normal. The weather was superb. We used a ladder to get in and out of the boxcar. When we moved, the ladder was placed across the open door. So you could sit by it and look at the landscape. Not that there was much to look at. The country between Crimea and central Ukraine is an immense steppe without a single tree. It is marvelously fertile. For ages it was Russia's bread basket until forced collectivization practically ruined the agriculture.

One trivial incident stuck in my memory. We stopped at a tiny station. I don't know why. There were no passengers getting either on or off since the train was not a regularly scheduled one. It was a freight train carrying something (we didn't know what) north. Our car was hitched on to it. The station was not one where the engines were changed. But there was the station and the stationmaster in front of the waiting room. Father and two or three other men lowered the ladder and went out to stretch their legs by walking up and down. And to our surprise a bell rang—just one stroke. Mother appeared in the doorway calling to father to get on board. Father laughed and said, "What's the hurry? It's only the first bell." Then came the two strokes. Mother became nervous, "Come, don't be silly, come on in." Three bells. Father: "There is still time. Now comes the whistle, then the long and short toots..." But by this time mother was near hysteria. Father jumped in followed by the others and pulled in the ladder just in time for the final toot. It was unlike him to tease like this, but I think he was in an elated mood ever since we left the miserable peninsula.

We kept going. Our top speed must have been 20 versts (about 14 miles) per hour. The engine was fed by lumber. Sometimes lumber dwindled, and some of us had to forage, mostly pulling boards out of deteriorating fences. Another difficulty was with upgrade. The train stopped. People had to get off and push. When I say "off," I mean it literally. People traveling on freight trains (illegally) sat on the roof or else on bumpers between cars rather than inside cars. They were tolerated by the crew, partly on humanitarian grounds, but also because they were useful when the engine couldn't make a grade. Then they got off and pushed. They did it willingly enough. They didn't cherish the idea of getting stranded in the steppe. So they made a terrific effort and the train started moving. Once it was moving, continued effort increased the speed.

Finally the top was reached. The whistle blew again signifying that it was all right to get aboard. The descent was as much fun as a toboggan ride.

The final stretch to Lozovaya was all downhill. We made it at night. The train was going faster than ever before. One old woman in our group, who had some unfortunate experience in Lozovaya, became hysterical, insisting that the town was cursed and that the train would crash. But we made it all right, found no vehicle at the station, walked with our baggage to grandpa's house, woke up the household and joined in the orgy of embracing and kissing.

We arrived during the last days of Passover. We missed the Seder, but grandpa arranged a special one just for me. I was the center of attention, having turned from an 8-year-old into a 10-year old. And, as one can imagine, we did a lot of eating. We had forgotten that there was such a thing as sour cream, not to mention eggs, beef and chicken. I spent a lot of time with Pasha, mother's youngest sister, and my favorite aunt.

After a couple of weeks the mood became somber. At times I saw mother in tears. I couldn't bring myself to ask them what the matter was. Once father said that mother was ill, and was worried about her. Finally I asked Pasha what was going on, and she told me.

She said that at mother's insistence, we were not going back to Crimea. Because of what I lived through during the last months in Crimea, I wasn't particularly eager to go back there myself. Then Pasha explained that father was given only a month's leave, so that he had to go back to his job there or else he might be arrested and punished. I asked whether mother knew about this. If she did, how could she insist that we not go back? Then Pasha told me about what mother had in mind. She thought it might be possible to leave Russia and go to America.

That put the matter into an entirely different light. I wanted to know what the argument was about. Didn't father want to go to America? His mother, some brothers and sisters were there. Pasha said it wasn't so simple. It might take several months to get out of the country and in the meantime father could be found and arrested, and who knows what would happen to him.

Father and mother had several talks about this. By and by Pasha explained to me what was being planned. My uncle Misha had met a young woman in western Ukraine just before he was taken prisoner and fell in love with her. Her name was Betty. After the war he looked her up, they were married, and settled in Satanov, a Jewish *stetl* on the Ukrainian-Polish border. Mother insisted that instead of returning to starving Crimea we go there. It was unlikely the authorities would look all over the country for father. We could live in Satanov waiting for an opportunity to cross the border into Poland and emigrate to America from there.

So that was the plan. Father finally came around. I suspect he hesitated not so much because of loyalty to his job in the Department of Education in Feodosia but because of his ambivalence about America.

CHAPTER

13

THE STETL

We head west toward Poland and, perhaps, freedom. We travel through the Pale, the region to which most Jews were confined during the czarist regime, the country of the stetls made famous by the Broadway play Fiddler on the Roof. *For those living in the Pale, however, this was no musical entertainment. It was a state of mind, a state of being and a way of life.*

WE TRAVELED AT FIRST IN PASSENGER TRAINS, but the journey was more complicated and less comfortable than the trip from Feodosia to Lozovaya in the freight train. The first leg was the short trip from Lozovaya to Kharkov. Mother told me about how Dr. Trinkler operated on my angioma nine years previously. She hadn't been there since. We spent a whole day on a platform between tracks waiting for a train to Kiev. The trip to Kiev, however, was almost normal like a trip in peacetime, father said. He timed the speed of the train by checking the time between verst signs. He said we were doing 60 versts (that's about 40 miles) per hour.

In Kiev we stopped for a few days with some distant relatives on the Babinsky side of the family. Then to Zhmerinka, a transfer station, again several hours waiting for a train going west. Then to Proskurov, the site of a major pogrom in 1919, where two of my grandmother's brothers were killed. That was as far as the railroad system reached. In Proskurov we hired a horse and wagon to take us to Satanov, traveled all day and got there at night. We stayed a few days at the Schwarzburgs, uncle Misha's in-laws. He and aunt Betty had no room to take us in.

In a few days we found a family who took us in as roomers. They had two children, one a girl about 17 or 18, the other a 6-year-old boy. The girl could speak, read and write Russian. She was plodding along the "thorny but well-marked path," expecting to take successive examinations for so many *gymnasia* classes. There was no point to it. It was unlikely that the *gymnasia* in Kamenetz-Podolsk, the nearest provincial city, still existed, but she continued on. What else was there to do? I don't know who tutored her. At the time we came she had no tutor. That was an opportunity. Father offered to tutor her, for which she and her parents were touchingly grateful, and a most cordial and warm relationship was established.

Father and mother, of course, spoke Yiddish, but a different dialect was spoken in that part of the country. People were amused by the way father and mother talked and were not discreet about their amusement. I remember one incident that caused much merriment. It was summer. There was a beautiful tree in front of the house, with ripe plums on it. Mother was sitting in its shade reading. A man came along and pointing at the tree asked in a matter-of-fact way,

"Se kabelukhes?"

Mother had no inkling what he was talking about. She ventured to guess that he was asking whether some one named Kabelukhes lived in the house. So she said,

"Nayn, du voint Liebman." (No, this is Liebmans' house.)

The man was astonished. He must have thought mother was deaf or feebleminded. He was referring to the tree and asking whether the plums were of the "kabelukhes" variety, much esteemed in those parts. (Mother had never heard of that variety.) This incident was a subject of lively conversation among the townspeople for many days afterwards.

Altogether, the manners of the inhabitants of Satanov were anything but reserved. Mother told how she asked someone where the post office was. She asked a woman on the street, trying her best to imitate the local pronunciation and inflection. The answer she got was "Why do you want to go there?"

The Liebmans had a boy, whom I undertook to teach Russian. I knew a smattering of Yiddish and soon knew enough words to communicate with him. I taught him to read by the Russian method, that is "by syllables."

The structure of Russian words is somewhat like that of Italian or Japanese: consonant-vowel, consonant-vowel. There are also successions of consonants, but they are not nearly so frequent as those in Czech or Polish. For example, the Czech word for finger is *prst,* the word for death is *smrt.* Russian has no such words. Take the Russian word for dog, *sobaka,* which is consonant-vowel-consonant-vowel-consonant-vowel. Or raspberry, *malina.* Get the picture? So Russian kids first learn letters, then syllables. Then they put syllables together and spell words. In learning to read, they name the syllables out loud. For example learning to read *sobaka* (dog), they say "s,o—so, b,a—ba, k,a—ka; so-ba-ka." now they can read "dog."

And that's also the way Jewish children learned to read Hebrew. So Shima and I had something in common, an important foundation for communication and learning.

I showed him the Hebrew letter "shin" (which he already knew, since he went to Hebrew school). It looks like the Russian letter "sha" and is pronounced the same way (sh). Then I showed him the Russian letter that is pronounced "ee". And told him to combine "sh" with "ee" to get "shee." Next I showed him "m" and "a" (pronounced "ah") which together form "ma." Then putting "shee" and "ma" together he got the sound of his name—Shima. He was delighted. And then when he combined "ma" with another "ma," he got "mama" (which has the same meaning in many languages). He ran to his mother to show her what he learned. Within a few weeks he could read the *bukvar* (first reader Russian).

My experience with other Jewish children was unfortunate. The *stetl* was the typical Jewish community in the southwestern part of the Pale, the region of the Russian empire where Jews were permitted to live without restrictions. They could not live either in the country or in the large cities except with special permission, for instance, if they were craftsmen, or had a profession, or were merchants with a certain minimum capital.

The *stetl* was made famous by Sholom Aleichem, the Jewish Gogol, and introduced to the general public in America by the Broadway musical *Fiddler on the Roof,* an adaptation of several of Sholom Aleichem's stories.

The connection between Sholom Aleichem and Gogol was that both masterfully portrayed the life of "little people"—the impoverished and the humble. And the title of the musical refers to another great portrayer of the *stetl* life—Marc Chagall.

Chagall was a painter. His style of painting anticipated that of the Spanish painter Salvador Dali. It is called "surrealism." If you are interested in art and get a chance to see an exhibit of Salvador Dali's paintings (such exhibits are often a traveling show visiting many countries), you will understand what "surrealism" is all about and also why the musical based on Sholom Aleichem's stories is called *Fiddler on the Roof*. You will also see the connection between *Fiddler on the Roof* and *Skating on Thin Ice*.

Dali liked to paint "melting" watches, for example, watches hanging limply on branches of trees. You might call Chagall the Jewish Salvador Dali. Chagall's paintings can also be called "surrealistic." He painted people and goats flying over the humble huts of a *stetl*. He also painted a man playing a fiddle on a roof, symbolizing the precariousness of *stetl* life.

The fiddle is a symbol of Jewish musicality. The great violinists of the first decades of the 20th century, the Mishas, Yashas, Toshas, Yehudis, were child prodigies, all Jews who remained world-class musicians all their lives. In one of Sholom Aleichem's stories, the town fiddler introduces a boy in love with the violin to the history of the instrument, his version of it, that is.

"The fiddle, you understand, is an instrument that is older than all other instruments. The first fiddler was Tubal Cain or Methuselah, I am not sure which. You may know, you study such things in *heder*. The second fiddler was King David. The third was a man named Paganini, also a Jew. The best fiddlers have always been Jews. I can name a dozen. Not to mention myself ... They say I don't play badly, but how can I compare myself with Paganini?

Paganini, we are told, sold his soul to the devil for a fiddle. He never would play for the great of this world—the kings and the princes—no matter how much they paid him. He preferred to play to the common people in taverns and the villages, or even in the woods to the beasts and birds. Ah, what a fiddler Paganini was!"

All this somehow hangs together with the spirit of Sholom Aleichem's and Gogol's stories. Gogol's genius was revealed in his feeling for tragi-comedy—laughing through tears. So was Sholom Aleichem's. Many of his stories are monologues. A Jew (usually a *kaptzen,* that is, next to a beggar) is telling Sholom Aleichem all about his *tsores* (troubles). The way he tells them sounds hilariously funny, but underneath this fun is profound tragedy. Both Gogol and Sholom Aleichem wrote about "little people," who tried to preserve at least a semblance of self-respect, which was almost an insurmountable task.

Fiddling on the roof symbolizes precariousness, constant danger. When Roger Rapoport, my cousin once removed, proposed *Skating on Thin Ice* as the title of this book, I thought it was an allusion to *The Fiddler on the Roof.* To be sure, when my parents decided to leave Russia they didn't know how precarious our situation was. We only learned about it in retrospect. I told how my father was arrested by the Whites and let go, when he convinced them that he wasn't a Soviet spy. It is practically certain that eventually he would have been arrested by the Reds, and you may be sure that they wouldn't let him go. Eventually, an arrested intellectual was marked for destruction either by hard labor or by a bullet in the back of the head.

One might ask "Why?" One might as well ask why the Nazis

killed six million Jews. The Holocaust puts other similar atrocities in the shadows. But one might ask why the Nazis killed all the Gypsies they could catch. Why did they kill the mentally ill? For that matter why did Hitler order all the members of his own street fighting battalion, the *Sturmabteilung,* shot when they were all assembled at a convention on June 30, 1934?

I think George Orwell understood why. As he pointed out in his great novel *Nineteen Eighty-Four,* one doesn't seize power in order to make a revolution; one makes a revolution in order to seize power. Power is not means to an end. Power is an end in itself. And the surest way to convince oneself that one has power is to destroy, to smash, above all to kill. Stalin, who succeeded in concentrating absolute power over a vast empire in his person, kept proving his omniscience to himself by destroying, dismantling, liquidating and killing. He had practically all of Lenin's closest collaborators shot, that is all those who weren't lucky enough to die in their own beds in time. And high on his hit list were the *intelligentsia* (the word has been adopted in English), people not only educated but also devoted to ideas and always eager to talk and argue about their ideas and ideals. They valued the freedom to think, sometimes more than their lives. Father was of the *intelligentsia* in this sense. So now it should be clear why father could not have possibly survived in Russia, at least not by the 1930s when the slaughter of the *intelligentsia* went into high gear.

In 1934, my cousin Volodya, my first playmate when I was 3 and he was 2, was exiled to Central Asia for making a remark. He was separated from his wife and 1-year-old son (named after me), whom he never saw again. After his three years of exile, he was sentenced to 10 years of hard labor in the Arctic for making another remark. He told me about this when we saw each other 50 years after we parted. They had amateur theatricals in Tashkent, the city in Central Asia to which he was exiled. They played *Servant of Two Masters,* an 18th-century French comedy. Volodya was the emcee, so he was making the curtain speech. He had a wry sense of humor. "Comrades and citizens," he said, "We are going to play *Servant of Two Masters.* In fact, I myself am, in a way, a servant of two masters: on the one hand (... something, I forget), and on the other (something else)," and so on in this tone. So when they told him that he was getting a "tenner," as the standard 10-year-sentence was called in those days, it was because he insinuated that there were servants and masters in the Soviet Union, and that came under the infamous Section 58 of the criminal code ("Slandering the Soviet Union").

Here is the way Sholom Aleichem describes the Jewish *stetl:*

"Stuck away in a corner of the world ... remote from the noise and bustle, which men have created about them and have dignified with high-sounding names like Culture, Progress, Civilization... not only do they know nothing of automobiles, ... airplanes; for a long time they refused to believe in the existence of the old ordinary rail road train... But it happened once that a householder in Kasrilevka had to go to Moscow. When he came back he swore with many oaths that it was true. He, himself had ridden in a train... He showed them how the wheels turned, the smokestack whistled, the carriages flew and people rode to Moscow. The people of Kasrilevka listened... and nodded their heads solemnly, and deep in their hearts they laughed at him. 'What a story! The wheels turn, the smokestack whistles, the carriages fly and people ride to Moscow and come back again!'

"If you ask them (the Kasrilevkites) 'How do you live?' they will answer with a shrug and a laugh, 'How do we live? Who knows? We live!' A remarkable thing, whenever you meet them, they are scurrying like rabbits, this one here, this one there. They never have time to stop. You ask them 'What are you hurrying for?' 'What am I hurrying for? Well, it's like this. If we hurry we think we might run into something—earn a few pennies, provide for the Sabbath.'

"To provide for the Sabbath—that is their goal in life. All week they labor, sweat, wear themselves out, live without food or drink, just so there is something for the Sabbath. And when the holy Sabbath arrives, let Yehupetz perish, let Odessa be raised, let Paris sink into the earth! Kasrilevka lives! And this is a fact that since Kasrilevka was founded, no Jew has gone hungry there on the Sabbath. Is it possible that there is a Jew who does not have fish for the Sabbath? If he has no fish, then he has meat. If he has no meat, herring. If he has no herring, then he has white bread. If he has no white bread, then he has black bread and onions. If he has no black bread and onions, then he borrows from his neighbor. Next week the neighbor will borrow from him. 'The world is a wheel and it keeps turning.' The Kasrilevkite repeats this maxim, and he shows you with his hand how it turns."

As I read these lines years later in America, I nodded as I read them. Of course I didn't see the life around me in Satanov as clearly as Sholem Aleichem saw his imaginary Kasrilevka, but I heard father and mother exchanging their impressions and they saw Satanov in the same light. The town was completely isolated. Life went on there as if the revolution had not occurred. It wasn't until winter that the Soviet presence made itself felt and the title of this book became relevant to our escape from what ultimately became the far less publicized Holocaust.

If someone asked me how we lived in Satanov, the *stetl* on the River Zbruch, I would answer like a Kasrilevkite, "We lived!"

Food was plentiful. Everything was sold in the open air market. Peasants came in with their wagons. Live poultry cackled and quacked in cages. Live fish swam in barrels. There was everything: eggs, milk, cottage cheese, the fruit season. Money was of two kinds: Polish marks and czarist 25-ruble notes with Empress Katerina II on it. These were called *Katerininki*. The Polish marks were the first Polish currency introduced when partitioned Poland became united as an independent state. There was something curious about these two currencies. The Polish marks were accepted in any condition, even bills torn in two and pasted together. But the *Katerininkis* were accepted only in mint condition. This seems strange, since bills that looked brand new were likely to be counterfeit. But there it was. Money has power if and only if people believe in it. And the Satanovites evidently believed in the Polish marks and in the image of Katerina II. I admit she looked majestic and could not be easily suspected of fraud.

We must have used that money, but how we got it, I confess I don't know. My parents may have had savings before the rev-

olution, and czarist money may still have been in use, or perhaps the Kerenki issued by the Provisional Government, which
came curiously in 20-ruble and 40-ruble notes. They may have
had some jewelry. Father did some tutoring in Satanov in families who wanted their children to learn Russian and go through
the standard *gymnasia* curriculum. Father even taught a little
English, to people who were dreaming of emigrating to
America some time. Anyway, I don't remember us being
strapped for money in Russia. In America was another matter.

I remember better how we spent our time. Father tutored
both me and Shima's sister. I taught Shima, my protégé.

I found it hard to relate to Jewish boys (except Shima). I
understood Yiddish, but didn't speak it. I tried for a while to
join them in their games (Shima was too young to go around
with them), but this led eventually to an unpleasantness.

I confess it was my own fault. I tried to show off, possibly as
compensation for my clumsy Yiddish, which the boys laughed
at. There was an abandoned factory on the edge of town and a
free-standing chimney about 30 feet tall. Inside the chimney
was a semblance of a ladder, that is, bent iron bars fixed into
the walls. One could climb on them. Once, when I was teased,
I boasted that I could climb up to the top of the chimney on
those bars. The more they laughed, the more I insisted and
finally I started up. I was scared, but giving up was out of the
question. I reached the top, emerged from the chimney to my
shoulders and waved triumphantly. There was no one below! I
started down again, which was much harder than going up
(the next rung down was harder to find). I was both scared and
furious. When I emerged, the boys came out from behind the
chimney, where they had hidden, seized me and held tight

until they smeared my mouth with goat droppings. "Take that for eating *khazr,*" they shouted.

At home I kept quiet about the incident. (I couldn't very well tell about climbing the chimney.) I found other companions, Ukrainian boys (one was Polish). Russian, Ukrainian and Polish were spoken, often mixed. We had no difficulty understanding each other.

Throughout the summer, father and I went to the dam adjoined to the abandoned water mill. The river spilled over the dam and formed a magnificent shower. Occasionally, father swam for a while. In spite of frequent trips to the beach in Feodosia, I had not learned to swim. But I had fun splashing around. I didn't realize at the time that this dam would be the focus of a book I would be writing 79 years later.

The summer waned. High holidays came and went. It was then that I discovered mother's absence. This was only the second time; the first time was in Feodosia when she was hospitalized for a few days. But there was no hospital in Satanov. It was then that father had no choice but explain the situation. Mother crossed over to Poland. She was going to make preparations for our emigration to America. When she was finished, she would come back and we would all go. In the meantime, he said emphatically, I mustn't say a word to anyone about this. If people asked me where mother is, I should say she went to Proskurov to visit some relatives. The Liebmans, of course, knew the state of affairs, as did uncle Misha, Betty and the Schwarzburgs.

Weeks passed, then months. No word from mother. I asked father questions but got only feeble reassurances. Finally, in December a stranger came (who later turned out to be the smuggler who helped us across) bringing a note from mother. She was just on the other side of the river. She wrote that we must now manage to cross somehow. But how? I saw father talking to the man but couldn't hear what was being said. Finally, the man left. Father told me we had to move to another house, and that I was not to talk about it to anyone. In fact, I was not to go out of the house to which we were moving.

That night the man came with horse and wagon. We loaded our belongings and without saying goodbye to our hosts, who were asleep, got into the wagon. There were blankets in the wagon. The driver told us to cover ourselves with them. The ride lasted only a few minutes. It stopped near a dilapidated house on a bluff overlooking the river. On the other side lay Poland and freedom.

CHAPTER

14

THE HOVEL ON THE BANK OF THE ZBRUCH: EXODUS

Why crossing the river Zbruch was a turning point in my life.
The last nine days in the country of my birth.

WE WERE MET BY AN OLD WOMAN who led us to a couple of straw mats side by side covered with old torn blankets. Father and I put our things beside the mats and lay down on them without undressing. There was a chamber pot beside the mats.

I fell asleep. When I woke up, the sun was shining through a window near the entry door. The hovel was just one big room. There was a partition behind which the parents slept. The old woman, probably a grandmother, and several kids slept on mats all over the place. There was a big table in the middle of the room for meals. There also was a Russian wood-burning oven for baking and a range for frying.

I don't remember how many kids there were, of all ages from a baby on. The kids all went to *heder* except the baby and two or three of the youngest. So during the day it was relatively quiet. But when the kids returned from *heder* late in the afternoon, the place was bedlam, but a cheerful bedlam. The kids made terrific noise, but I don't remember much crying or quarrelling. I remember one game in particular where kids in turn yelled *reekhes!* I knew it meant "devils," but that's all I could make out of the games. I think I tried to join once or twice, but the kids were shy. Father told me to leave them alone. We kept to ourselves. We had books with us. I read.

The days went quickly. Father sometimes talked about America. He was looking forward to seeing his mother, whom he hadn't seen since he was there in 1907. It was not to be, however. The first thing he learned when we were finally reunited with mother was that his mother, grandma Fayga, had died in September. (Mother corresponded from Warsaw with uncle Mendel.)

I kept thinking of the film I saw in the heady days between the February and the October revolutions. It wasn't the first film I saw, but it made the deepest impression on me. I mentioned it—*The Cottage on the Bank of the Volga*. And here we were in a hovel on the bank of the Zbruch.

Recall the plot of that movie. An arrested revolutionary escapes and is taken in by a family, hiding out until the czarist regime is overthrown. And here was father, also a revolutionary at heart, taken in by a family, hiding out until he can cross the border to freedom. Both refuges are on a bluff overlooking a river. The Russians call the Volga the mother of rivers. The Zbruch is only a stream, but it marks the border between constant danger and relative security. Sounds a little far-fetched, but I was still under Sonya's influence. Her imagination and inclination to romanticize trivial parallels must have rubbed off on me.

Days passed and no word from the smuggler. Father was

getting desperate. Suppose it proves impossible to cross? Suppose someone informs on us, father is arrested, and I am taken to an orphanage? Mother is relatively safe, that is, unless the Polish border police find her and recall that she once escaped from them. But even if she manages to get to America somehow, what will her life be like when she finds out what happened to us? I think these images drove father to concoct the foolish scheme—sending me to skate across the river.

I had skates and I could skate a little. The skates were not mine. The Polish boy, with whom I was most friendly, lent them to me when he was teaching me to skate. Father wouldn't ever let me skate on the river, that is, before he got desperate. There were large frozen puddles all over Satanov and a duck pond. That's where I learned.

Somehow, when we packed, we took those skates. Maybe it was when they turned up in the hovel that father got the idea. He explained what should be done. He said he saw kids skating near the Polish shore right next to the dam of the water mill. That was the dam on which mother had crossed. It was some hundred yards down the river, to the south of the hovel. Early one morning, he took me outside to the windowless wall of the hovel and showed me where the dam was.

He explained what had to be done. He would watch till kids appeared near the other shore skating on the river. When they did, I was to go down the bluff to the shore, put on the skates and skate across to join those kids. If they asked me questions I was to say something in Ukrainian to distract them. Anyway, there was little chance that they would notice me. There were usually at least 20 of them skating. The other bank was not steep near the dam.

The skates were not attached to the shoes as they are now. They were screwed on.

In fact, even in America back then the skates were not attached to shoes. They had clamps and were screwed on with a key.

When I got across, I was to take off the skates and walk down the river, that is, with the river on my left, till I came to the third cottage. That's where mother was. I was to explain the situation to her. She would then decide whether to wait for father, on the chance that he could cross in a few days, or for us to go back to Warsaw without him, hoping that he could somehow manage to escape later.

It was a bright and sunny morning, I think between 9 and 10 o'clock. There was a fence along the river that hid it from view. I walked along it carrying the skates till I came to a break in the fence. Looking through the gap I saw the crowd of kids skating near the opposite shore. I also saw the dam, apparently with no one on it. I went down the bluff, sat down on the snow and screwed on the skates. I kept looking at the dam. Still no one on it. I estimated the distance to the kids. It was considerably more than the length of the duck pond, but I thought I could easily skate across. I had to, anyway.

So, I kept repeating to myself. Skate across, shake off the skates, leave them and run down the river. Third cottage. Mother is there. If she isn't, explain to the people who I am. They will know. Wait for mother.

I started out. I kept thinking: the ice holds near the shore, otherwise the kids wouldn't be skating there; will it hold in the middle of the stream? Should I go slowly or as fast as I can?

Suddenly I heard a shout. There was a Red Army man on

the dam. He was shouting and waving at me. Then he aimed his rifle at me. I turned around and skated back as fast as I could. I thought no more about whether the ice would hold. All I thought of was to get back to the Russian side.

I forgot all about the break in the fence. I didn't see it when I climbed up the bank, probably because I had gone out on a diagonal but coming back went straight for the shore. All I remember is that somehow I climbed over that fence and sat panting on the other side. Then I saw our hovel on the bluff up the river and went there. I found father in panic. He grabbed me and, I think, he sobbed. After that I didn't venture out of the hovel.

I don't recall how many nights after that the smuggler reappeared. A Red Army man was with him. The first thing he said was, "Who is to go across?" I thought this was the end, that he had come to arrest us. But father went up to him and they talked for some time.

Finally the Red Army man said, "Remember now. If we get caught, I'll say that I have arrested you and am taking you to headquarters. It won't make any difference to you and at least I'll save my skin."

Then I saw father handing him some money—Polish marks. We went out and walked along the bluff up the river in the direction away from the dam. There was a bend and beyond it the dam was out of sight. It didn't make any difference at night, but that's the way the escape had been planned, so that's the way we went.

We descended down from the bluff and started across on the ice. I was carrying a pair of shoes, which for some reason were not packed with the other things. One of them fell, but I didn't dare stop to pick it up. Clearly the other shoe alone was useless, but I didn't think of that either and kept carrying it.

There was a bluff also on the other side. We started climbing it. A man came down and gave me a hand. Then we walked away from the river and walked on a road down the river. We must have passed the dam, but I didn't see it. Finally we came to a hut. Our guide, not the smuggler (he was gone) but the man who helped us when we crossed, knocked on the door. The door opened, we went in, and there was mother grabbing me and weeping. The next thing I remember is father sobbing. Mother told him that grandma died. Many years later father told me that he felt guilty for years for having ignored his mother's pleas to stay in America and kept hoping he would see her again and atone for having left her.

We didn't tarry in the hut. A wagon and a driver stood ready. We were on the way. There was still a last hurdle. A Polish soldier stopped us on the way. I saw father giving him Polish 100 mark bills, one after the other until, he said, he had no more. So the soldier let us go. I rather think that the soldier was in on the whole thing, that is that he collaborated with smugglers and got his cut when an occasion arose.

It was probably near midnight when we got to the station. I told father how to say "Two third class to Lvov and one child" in Polish. I told him to pronounce Lvov "Lvoov," the way it sounds in Polish. The Ukrainian pronunciation is "Lveev." It wouldn't do for father to speak Ukrainian. All Ukrainians in those parts on both sides of the river were peasants. Father didn't look like a peasant. He wore city clothes. A disguise wouldn't help if he had to talk. He didn't sound like a peasant. He could (hopefully) pass for a city Pole. That's why it was best for him to ask for tickets in Polish.

We were lucky. A train came within minutes. In the compartment mother took out some bread and sausage and we ate. It was then that I noticed how hungry I was.

15

POLAND

In Poland a new life begins with a family in the Jewish quarters.

A FEW DAYS AFTER WE CROSSED THE BORDER, we got to Warsaw, where we found lodging with a family in the Jewish quarter. Under Nazi occupation the quarter became the infamous ghetto, razed after the desperate uprising of the Jews throwing bottles with burning gasoline at tanks.

Our home was in an apartment on the fourth floor (walk-up) of a huge slum building. The apartment consisted of a living-dining room, bedroom, kitchen and toilet. There was no bath. To bathe one went to public baths. Lighting was by gas. The gas stank as a precaution against poisoning in case it leaked.

The Fromberg family, with whom we shared the apartment, consisted of a couple in their 40s, a 15-year-old daughter, a 10-year-old daughter, an 8-year-old son and a grandmother. The host couple slept on a couch in the main room. My parents slept in one bed in the bedroom. The boy and I slept in another. The two girls slept in a third. The grandmother slept in the kitchen. There was only one exit and no fire escape.

The children came home from school in mid-afternoon, and the whole family, including us had dinner. The dinner was quite good. The family kept kosher. After dinner all the children did their homework. The younger children, Andzia and Pawelek, finished around 5 or 6 o'clock. But the eldest, whose name I don't recall, worked through the evening, sometimes till bedtime.

We seldom went out. When we did, I was impressed by the city. Baku was also a large city but definitely Oriental. Warsaw was a European city. In addition to horse-drawn cabs, there were motor taxis. The streetcars were electric, not horse-drawn as in Baku. Stores had window displays. There were palaces and imposing buildings. The river Vistula was spanned by bridges.

At home I played with Andzia and Pawelek (having quickly learned some Polish, which is akin to both Ukrainian and Russian). I terribly missed Sonya, with whom I had intimate contact during our last two months in Feodosia. I thought the eldest Fromberg daughter might take her place. She was quite cordial to me but much too busy with her studies and household chores.

Pawelek, like the boys on Italian Street in Feodosia, was primarily interested in war. I had enough of war, but I humored him. In his opinion, the best warriors in the world were the Germans (Warsaw had been occupied by the Germans during World War I). Perhaps in the interest of maintaining cordial relations, he assured me that the Russians were also great fighters, almost as great as the Germans. He expected the next great war to be between the "yellow race" and the Europeans. He must have heard about the "yellow peril," which was still a rampant idea in the early decades of the century. In that war the Russians and the Germans, he said, would play a leading role in defending Europe.

My relations with Andzia were quite different. She was sensitive about people and spoke freely about them. She told me how she felt about her brother and sister and asked me whether I had any siblings. I told her I didn't and wished she were one. She wanted to know what I was going to be when I grew up. That was a brief period when I had delusions of grandeur. I read a science fiction story about a latter-day imitator of Jules Verne's Captain Nemo, who built a combination of submarine, airship and land vehicle and used it to enforce social justice throughout the world. Andzia loved fantasy and in this way reminded me of Sonya. But with Andzia my relations were the reverse of what they were with Sonya: I was the mentor, she the disciple.

Twelve years later I came to Warsaw to give a piano recital. I looked forward eagerly to seeing the family again. I remembered the address: Twarda 23, apartment 48 on the fourth floor. I knocked on the door. No answer. I remembered a neighbor just below on the third floor. I knocked. This time the door opened, and the neighbor, whom I recognized by his wall-eye, looked at me.

I named myself.

"Rapoport! But you are so young!" he cried in Yiddish. He took me for my father.

I explained and inquired about the Frombergs. They moved to the country, he said, managing some summer resort. Yes, he could give me the address of the eldest daughter.

She was sincerely glad to see me. She had been to America, tried to settle in New Jersey. The life was awful during the Depression. She came back to Warsaw and was now married.

I inquired about Andzia and Pawelek.

Pawelek was doing fine. He was a student at the university. She evaded my questions about Andzia. Finally she told me. Andzia was in the Communist underground. She could arrange for me to see her, but only on a busy street. I went where she directed me and met the 23-year-old Andzia. Our conversation flagged. I couldn't talk about myself unless she asked, and she didn't. And I couldn't ask her to tell me about herself, because I had promised her sister that I would not. So finally, I pecked her on the cheek, and she caught a streetcar.

Unless this family managed to escape to the Soviet Union, they all must have perished in the Holocaust.

Coming back to 1922, about March or April, we had to move from Warsaw to Wolomin, a near-by village, now incorporated into Warsaw. It was about a half-hour by rail from Praga, a suburb across the Vistula River. All our applications for immigration to America were done. It remained to wait for the visa. Father would go to Warsaw once or twice a week to inquire at the consulate and to buy some delicatessen. I found some friends, all from families who fled from Russia in various ways and were waiting to be admitted as immigrants wherever they were heading for.

You can see me with three of those friends on the photo. One of them was Misha Richter, several of whose cartoons appeared in the New Yorker in the 1930s. When I saw the signature, I wondered whether that was the Misha whom I knew in Wolomin, and he turned out to be the one.

My meeting with Shura Raskin (to my right on the photo) was more dramatic. The Raskins did not go to America. They went to Brussels and got caught in the Holocaust when the Germans invaded Belgium. As they were being transported in

*Above: second boy—Shura Raskin
third boy—author*

*Right: Raskin and author in same position
28 years later in Berchtesgaden near the
ruins of Hitler's villa*

freight cars to the concentration camps, Shura managed to escape and survived in hiding. When the Americans came, he offered his services to intelligence and was engaged by the OSS, later the CIA. I got wind of him through my parents' friends, whom we knew in Wolomin and who were living in New York. When Gwen and I got married in 1949, we went to Europe on our honeymoon (six months after the wedding). I found Shura in Munich. He was now working for a committee engaged in helping the Holocaust survivors to get settled. As you can imagine, we talked a lot. There was much to talk about. Shura took Gwen and me to Berchtesgaden, where Hitler had his mountain retreat. The villa was now in ruins. In the photograph you can see Shura and me in the same position as in the Wolomin photograph. It was taken next to the ruins of Hitler's villa.

Back to Wolomin. One day father came back from Warsaw with the usual supply of delicatessen and other goodies. On each package was scribbled "The visa has arrived!"

In two days we were ready. Back to Warsaw to board an international train. I remember crossing the German border in the early evening. I felt I was really abroad now. Poland didn't count. It was actually only an extension of Russia, was, in fact part of Russia a few years ago. But Germany! That was really *zagranitsa,* the West, a fabulous world of high civilization. Beyond Germany was Belgium, beyond Belgium, France, then the great ocean, then America!

The thrill continued. In Paris we spent a whole day, hired a taxi to see the sights: Place de la Concorde (where the guillotine used to stand), the Arc de Triomphe, and, of course the Eiffel Tower, at the time the tallest structure in the world.

We spent a week in Le Havre waiting for our ship—*Paris* of

the French Line. We lived in dorms provided for third-class passengers. The crossing was rainy and stormy, but the last two days glorious. And finally we were sailing past the lady with the torch!

AMERICA

ALL THE IMMIGRANTS, that is practically all the third-class passengers, landed on Staten Island and went through a screening procedure. They were asked where they were bound, and who was to meet them. They were tested for contagious diseases. There was a literacy test. All adults had to show that they could read some language. Since the immigrants were overwhelmingly from Russia or Poland, not many interpreters were required. A man ahead of us was given a Russian newspaper. One headline began with "Anglia ..." (England). The man read just that word. Then the official pointed to another headline, "Why Is (some country, I forget which) Silent?" The man read that one, too, and was motioned to go on. I was happily looking forward to being examined and to telling them that I could read Russian, English and German. But the man didn't even look at me. He examined father. Father said he could read English, read a headline and was motioned to pass on.

The whole procedure took a few hours. A ferry took us to Manhattan. I forgot how we got to Grand Central Station. It couldn't have been by bus, because there were no buses in those days. At Grand Central, I remember father buying train tickets and embracing mother. I think she wept. We were on the way.

The coach was not at all like the coaches in Europe. There were no compartments. All seats faced in the same direction, so that one looked at the back of the seat ahead. However, the seats could be reversed, and the conductor reversed the one ahead of us, so that we could sit facing each other. We sat this way through the night and came to Buffalo early in the morning. There we were stuck. A railroad strike was on. We spent two days in the coach standing on a siding. It was just like waiting for an engine on our nine-day trip from Feodosia to Lozovaya.

We had telegraphed uncle Mendel from New York telling our expected time of arrival, and he kept phoning the station to inquire whether that train was already on the way and if so, when it was to arrive. Finally we were riding through Chicago's South Side. The train rushed past the local stations, which were all named by numbered streets—59th Street, 55th Street, 47th Street. The numbers were all diminishing. Father said that the terminal was at 12th Street. And so it was.

The next thing I remember is mother's elated shout, "Oy! Mendel!" She recognized him from a photograph. Yes, there was uncle Mendel and father's youngest sister, Aunt Ruth, in the last month of pregnancy and two of uncle Mendel's four daughters, Estelle, 14, and Sophie, 9. The eldest, Jean, was 16 and Doris was a baby. Jean is now 93, Estelle is 91, Sophie is dead and Doris is 78. Daniel, Roger Rapoport's father, was 6.

We got into two taxis, and I impressed aunt Ruth and cousin Estelle by speaking English. Uncle Mendel's apartment on the Northwest Side was over a garage, and because the garage extended farther back, there was a very large porch behind the kitchen. In summer some of the family slept on it. Soon after we arrived, most of the clan gathered at uncle Mendel's. One was a very tall young man. I saw father whispering something to him, as it turned out telling him to keep quiet when I was introduced to see whether I would recognize him. I did. It was uncle Niuma, who had visited us in Lozovaya in 1914 and left just before World War I broke out. When I called him by name, he grabbed me in his arms and started kissing me. On the whole, it was a most emotional reunion mostly for father, since mother hardly remembered any of the American relatives. Tears were shed over grandma's death a year before.

Just a few days after our arrival, father and mother started talking about bringing over the remaining two brothers, uncle Yania and his family and uncle Aron. Every one was willing to chip in. But the project didn't get very far. Within weeks after our arrival, we got terrible news. Anya, uncle Yania's eldest daughter, was missing. She was a student, majoring in geology. The class went on a field trip in the Crimean wilderness. She disappeared and was never found. Uncle Yania spent several days going over the paths followed by the expedition, hoping to find at least a trace of her—all in vain. The plans of bringing the family over were postponed. By the time all hope was given up, a new immigration law was passed, which made the reunion in the foreseeable future virtually impossible. In the early 1990s, Sonya, Volodya, Elena (Volodya's daughter) and her two sons, Anton and Peter, emigrated to Israel. Sonya and Volodya have since died. Elena and the two boys are the last contact I have with the Russian *meshpukhe*.

We spent two weeks at uncle Mendel's and two at uncle

Author aged 12 and his American cousins. Standing: Anita, Jean,
Estelle, author. Next row: Sophie, Daniel, Nat, Charlotte. Bottom row:
Nita, Leonard, Doris, Seymour.

Niuma's, then another month again at Uncle Mendel's before
we found our own place. It was just a bedroom in the flat
inhabited by a woman estranged from her husband, living with
her son about my age. Another bedroom was rented to a mid-
dle-age working woman. School started in September during
our second sojourn at uncle Mendel's.

It was in the first two months that my attitude toward life in
America set. Of course, it underwent changes through the
many decades, as I matured, passed through ideological crises,
grew old. But its basis remained: It was a repetition of my
father's disappointment with the "Promised Land" told in the
first chapter.

I now realize that my adoration of my cousin Sonya was a

childhood fixation. I also mentioned the eldest of the Fromberg girls, whom I thought might take Sonya's place but didn't and whom I looked up in Warsaw in 1933. Now it was Estelle, my 14-year-old cousin, whom I had my eyes on. She liked me well enough but there was no basis for the sort of relationship I longed for. As for Jean, the eldest, she was absorbed in taking both piano and organ lessons. But that was no bond. Her interests were exclusively practical. She planned to become an organist in a movie theater.

The silent movies of those days were always accompanied by music. In Russia, pianists filled that role. In America, at least in the big cities, it was organists. Although playing the organ seriously, that is, to play organ works of Bach, for example, requires serious musical know-how; just to make decent sounds on the organ takes no skill at all. Touch, the crucial pianistic skill, makes no difference on the organ. So it doesn't take years just to make acceptable sounds. If one played the piano, all one needed to be a movie organist was to acquire a basic repertoire: a few dozen salon pieces, marches (to accompany parades shown on news reels), jazz to accompany slapstick comedy or cartoons, sentimental songs, snatches of "ethnic" music to play when Germans, Italians, Jews or American Indians in Westerns appeared on the screen. There were special courses on "movie organ" in music schools, and that's the sort of training Jean meant to acquire. A movie organist was paid union scale—$60 per week, almost twice as much as father earned when he worked as a milkman. So there was no prospect of a serious bond between Jean and me.

However, there was Sophie. I saw her in the role of Andzia, my ersatz sister in Warsaw. We were fond of each other.

Author wearing a podiovka

Although she was two years my junior, she was a head taller. We walked to and from school together. We walked Russian fashion. Look at the photo taken in Wolomin—the four of us, Misha Richter, Shura Raskin, myself and a kid I don't remember. Do you see how we stand with our arms around each other's shoulders? That's the way pairs of Russian kids, male, female, or mixed walked, when they were friends.

I don't know whether they still walk that way. I doubt it. But they did when I was a child. Anyhow, the first culture shock I experienced was when mother took me aside and told me that Sophie came back from school in tears. Her girlfriends teased her about having a boy friend. Mother said it was all right to walk to school together but not with arms around shoulders.

So much for boy-girl relationships. Now for the male bonding. Once after school, as I was waiting by the gate for Sophie to appear, a boy deliberately stepped on my foot, made a face at me and went on. I was furious. I recalled Pawelek in Warsaw telling me that when American boys quarrel, they fight it out by boxing. Pawelek was a prize fight fan, knew all the past champions. He showed me how one boxed and what happens when a boxer is floored, how the referee counts over him, and if doesn't get up by the count of 10, the other boxer wins. We even played at boxing, arranging for one of us to be "knocked out" at exactly 10 p.m. so that the clock in the living room would provide the count. So when the boy deliberately provoked me, I thought this was a chance to show him that I know how one retaliates in America. I started to make boxing motions at him, as Pawelek had taught me. My enemy dealt me a fierce blow on the forehead. I ran sobbing home. My black and blue bump was bathed in cold water, and I was consoled, but I declared I wasn't going to school any more.

Soon after that we moved to our new quarters, and I was transferred to another school, promoted to fourth grade, soon after that to fifth. Cold weather set in. I looked forward to appearing in my *podiovka,* the ankle-length fur-trimmed coat, and explaining to my school mates that well-to-do Russians of the merchant class wore that sort of coat. Moments after I entered the school yard, I was surrounded by a mob of boys (boys and girls were segregated in the yard before school started and at recess).

"Look, he's wearing a girl's coat," they yelled. The bell rang, and I was rescued, but at recess I was mobbed again. At home I told my parents what happened. They were shocked. They asked me what the kids were wearing, meaning to get something suitable, but I wouldn't hear of it. I declared that I would wear nothing else. "Let those American boys beat me to death," I declared, "I'm Russian, and I will wear my Russian coat."

The upshot was that father went to see the principal. As a matter of fact, the matter had become known. The principal was very decent about it. The teachers were instructed to speak to their classes about the incident. They told the kids that America welcomed people from many countries, and that other countries had different customs and wore different clothes and that I was wearing the sort of coat men wore in the country I came from and that this was nothing to be teased about or to be ashamed of.

There was another incident in that same school that showed American attitudes toward immigrants in another light. I was already in eighth grade (I went through grammar school in a year). The eighth graders published a semester magazine written by them and also printed by them in the printing shop. (Trades were taught in elementary schools; at that time this was all the schooling most kids got). My English teacher impressed with my progress in English suggested that I write a story for the semi-annual magazine, entitled "Why and How I Came to America."

I wrote about the starvation in Crimea and about how we crossed the river on ice and about our trip over Europe and about the sea voyage and about how glad we were to be welcomed by our American relatives. The teacher said that was fine.

"And now," she continued, "tell how you like America." And I blurted out, "But I don't like America, Mrs. Garren, I want to go back to Russia." Mrs. Garren looked strangely at me. "You better ask your parents to help you with this," she said and dismissed me. At home father and mother told me that I shouldn't have said what I said. Father insisted on helping me write the ending. I resisted for a while but then gave up. Mrs. Garren was satisfied, and the story was published.

One might think that deep inside I felt very bad about the *podiovka* affair. But I really didn't at the time. I blurted out what I did for another reason. Once Mrs. Garren was talking about how America was a haven for the persecuted and about the meaning of liberty and so on. Then she asked, "How many of you children came here from the Old Country or have parents who came from there?" Practically every one raised their hands. Our neighborhood was populated almost exclusively by immigrant Jews or Poles.

Mrs. Garren nodded approvingly and said, "And we are very glad to have you here. I am sure all of you will become good Americans." Then she continued, "And do you know whom we don't like to come to America?" No one knew. "Japs," said Mrs. Garren. "More and more Japs come to America. They settle in California and buy up all the good land. They want to drive all the Americans out of California, so they can have it for their own."

That was in 1923, shortly after the Japanese Exclusion Act was passed in Congress. It was that incident I thought about when I blurted out my tactless remark that shocked Mrs. Garren.

My attitudes toward America were formed throughout my adolescence, that is until 1929 when I went to study music in Vienna. I came back in the depths of the Great Depression, found a very different country and people my age to whom I could easily relate. In many ways the 1930s were, like the 1960s, bright decades in American history, which I see in retrospect through the eyes of the young, but we won't go into that. Let me go on with the story of my late childhood.

In September 1923, I entered Murray F. Tuley High School on the near Northwest side. The student body was practically 100 percent Jewish. That was because the Polish kids went predominantly to trade schools. Tuley was a liberal arts school with a business two-year course for girls attached (short hand, typing, filing).

The teachers were mostly surprisingly good. They were of the older generation when high school was still regarded as an institution of higher learning and, perhaps, refined learning. In English classes students were still required to memorize poems or famous speeches. I remember particularly one old teacher who taught both English and chemistry. In English we studied Edmund Burke's famous speech on reconciliation with American colonies. We memorized poems of Milton and Wordsworth and soliloquies from Macbeth.

It was in the chemistry class that this teacher made an impression on me. He was an admirer of Lomonosov, the eighteenth-century Russian genius of humble birth who made major contributions in both philology and chemistry. He dismissed the antique dogma of the four elements (Earth, Air, Fire and Water) and of the "Quintessence" underlying all of them. He insisted that water was water not because of any "quintessence" but only because it has the properties of water, which were determined by the elements that composed it—hydrogen and oxygen. Any substance, Lomonosov insisted, is defined entirely and completely by its properties. In other words Lomonosov's reality consisted of observable events, not of imaginary principles.

The French teacher was a prig but entirely devoted to her subject. We read Maupassant's *My Uncle Jules* in French and even a French novel about a teenager who won a bet with his father that he could get along on his own.

In the Latin class (yes, Latin was taught in Tuley), we read Caesar's *Gallic Wars*. The teacher brought in a perfect model of the bridge that Caesar built across the Rhine and pointed out its features as we read about them in the text.

I met a boy my age, passionately devoted to music (he played the clarinet), and we organized a chamber ensemble from which I made arrangements and we played them at club meetings.

In other words, I found an environment in which intellectual life counted for something and people my age who lived it. I also became fond of Charlotte and Anita. Charlotte was sparkling and imaginative, reminding me of Sonya. Anita was serious, even somber on occasions and appealed to me in a way different from the way I loved Charlotte. Charlotte appreciated my enthusiasms for music, literature, drama (of this later) but was also a bon vivant. I remember her dating at an early age. I don't remember Anita dating. She seemed entirely absorbed in becoming a high-grade professional, which she did. My longing for a mentor like Sonya melted away. Both Charlotte and Anita were my equals. Still I realized sadly that deep friendship between boys and girls (without sexual overtones) practically did not exist in America. And that irked me.

Author aged 14

Now I come to events that made clear to me my absorption with Russia, which has lasted throughout my life. In 1923 the Moscow Art Theater came to Chicago. This theater was a legend in our family, that is, in the life of my parents and of mother's siblings. There was no hope whatever to see their productions in Moscow. They heard descriptions of them from people who managed somehow to get to Moscow and see them. Sheer magic. One felt that somehow one got inside the characters portrayed and lived their lives, suffered with them, rejoiced with them. The cast that came to Chicago was the original cast, put together by the founders, Stanislavsky and Nemerovich-Danchenko. Among them was Olga Knipper Chekhova, Chekhov's widow. It was the Moscow Art Theater that made Chekhov's plays world famous.

They repeated their visit in 1924. Altogether they did 11 plays. The three of us saw every one. At $3 per ticket, the total was $99.00. The money was borrowed and paid out in installments. It was then that I realized how much Russian culture meant to my parents and how they missed it.

Then there was uncle Niuma. He was the only one in the American branch of the family who spoke fluent Russian, and all three of us always spoke Russian with him. You will recall that he went to Russia in 1914 to register for the draft, because he didn't want to lose his Russian citizenship. He had a substantial Russian library about the same size as my parents' library left back in Russia. Soon after we came, I started to read the books. For four years I read almost exclusively Russian except for what was required in school.

Uncle Niuma had a record player—a Victrola it was called in those days—which you had to wind up by hand. And on them was the recorded voice of the fabulous Chaliapin, another family icon. In 1924 we heard him in concert. Most of the audience was Russian of course and the atmosphere was just like it was in Feodosia, when Smirnov sang there. When the program ended, no one left. The people kept calling for encores. At one point Chaliapin moved the grand piano to the footlights, sat down at it and sang a gypsy romance accompanying himself at the piano as Russian amateurs do. The audience went wild. I suppose Chaliapin was for the people of my parents' generation what Frank Sinatra was for my contemporaries and Elvis Presley for my children.

And then there was Rachmaninov. He came to Chicago, I believe, in 1925, the first great pianist I ever heard. And here is the way I found out that father, too, was longing for Russian culture. Somehow he arranged for the great pianist to see us. We went at the appointed time to the Auditorium hotel, where he stayed. Coming out of the elevator, we were met by a young man, either a secretary or a valet, who informed us that Sergei Vasilievich (that was Rachmaninov's name and patronymic) never auditions anyone. Actually that's what we came for, but there was nothing to be done. We assured the young man that we had no such intention. We were ushered in. I sill remember my surprise when I felt Rachmaninov's hand—not strong and dry, as I expected but soft, almost flabby. How could he make those granite-like sounds on the piano with hands like this? Rachmaninov asked what he could do for us.

Father said he hoped to learn something about the state of musical situation in Russia. He said he was told that I showed great promise and wondered whether I should be under tutelage of a great teacher.

Still there was a thought behind it that reveals his immersion in Russian culture. There was a belief in Russia, especially among Jews, that talented children of humble birth are "discovered" by some great musician, artist, scientist, what not, taken as a protégé and launched on a brilliant career. There is a story by the great Russian author Kuprin about a young boy making his living by playing dances at parties of the rich, who is "discovered" by Anton Rubinstein, the great Russian pianist of the 19th century.

I doubt that father shared that folk belief. Still it may have lurked somewhere in the back of his mind, and he brought up the subject of a "great teacher" to continue the conversation. At the time, I thought father still longed to return to Russia sometime, when the wounds of the revolution and the civil war were healed.

Rachmaninov said, "Why do you ask me this?"

Father said he thought Rachmaninov, being Russian, could tell him whether it was worthwhile to send me to Russia to study.

"I can't answer this question," said Rachmaninov. "Since I left Russia I severed all connections with it. If you wish me to recommend someone who can tell you whether it is worth-while for your son to pursue a musical career, I would recom-mend Alexander Siloti. I am sure he will give you an honest and well-founded opinion."

Siloti was in New York. There was as much chance of my going to New York as to Russia. There was nothing else to say. We thanked Sergei Vasilievich and left. So there it was. It seems father missed Russia, that is the Russia he imagined—a land of brilliant culture (to be sure on a miserable social foundation). He probably thought that the fruits of the revolution would eventually wash this rotten foundation away and create a new solid one.

Father knew some English but surely not enough to get a white-collar job. Continuing education was, of course, out of question. A living had to be made. His first job was working in a print shop on a night shift. It paid $15 per week. Then he was fortunate in getting a job as a milkman. Uncle Niuma was one and he got him the job. It paid good wages — union scale, $36 per week — but the work was hard. Milk was delivered by horse-drawn wagons during the night. Father had to get up at 2 a.m. to go to the barn where horses and wagons were kept, hitch up the wagon (he knew how this was done in Russia, but had to learn the American way) and drive over his delivery route.

Practically all apartment houses in Chicago had three stories (single houses were almost all in the suburbs). The milkman climbed the back stairs with baskets loaded with milk bottles and other dairy products as ordered, left them at the back doors and picked up the returned empty bottles. Often he found a note in the bottle asking for some other items (cream, cheese, etc.). If he didn't have it in the basket, he had to go back down and bring it up.

After the deliveries, father had to make the rounds again to collect money for a week's delivery. In those days, people of the working class knew nothing about checks, and they weren't given credit anyway. It was a good idea to chat with the house-wife awhile, to maintain goodwill and perhaps sell her some-thing in addition to the regular order.

Father's health was never robust. He finally quit. An oppor-tunity came up to buy a paper-delivering route in Oak Park, a middle-class suburb of Chicago. This, too, had to be abandoned for reasons that are of little relevance to my story. Father went back on the milk wagon. Then he ran a grocery store (this was in the days before the chain stores drove the small, family-run grocery stores out of business). He ended up as a successful business executive, but he was most unhappy in that role. I told you what father, along with other idealistic young Russian Jews, aspired to. Mother had the same aspirations, but when she mar-ried father she resigned herself to the role of homemaker.

I was unhappy, mostly because I felt for father, who, like Sonya, was my earliest mentor. Like him I was a socialist (except for a brief flirtation with communism in the late 1930s) and a pacifist (except when I served in the U.S. Air Force, believing that the alliance of the U.S. and U.S.S.R. would last and the two powers would establish and nourish a people-ori-ented world order). Like father, I had no use for the business world, no appetite whatsoever for making money. What I found among most boys my age with few exceptions (I learned enough to leave girls alone) was a fixation on diametrically opposed values, namely, competing and fighting. The most prominent heroes were heavyweight boxing champions. I remember a front page cartoon on the day of the bout between

champion Jack Dempsey and challenger Gene Tunney: grin-
ning Father Time covering up a portion of a front page headline—THE CHAMP IS (....)EY!.

Pugilists, cowboys pursuing cattle rustlers and Indians in
Saturday afternoon movies, were the role models among the vast
majority of my contemporaries. I despised the idol of violence.

The other idol I despised was money, in America the universal measure of competitive success. Recall the play *Satan,*
which we saw in Feodosia during its boom days. Satan almost
succeeds in corrupting the pious Jew by making him rich.

The contempt for (and at times fear of) money pervaded the
community, little known outside of Russia, called *intelligentsia.*
It is usually identified as comprising the educated, but this def-
inition does not capture its character. It's more accurate to say
that the *intelligentsia* consisted of people for whom ideas meant
much more than food, drink, sleep or sex, let alone money.

The *intelligentsia* despised appetite for money and people
who had an appetite for it. During the four decades preceding
the revolution, the hard core of the *intelligentsia* (as it was self-
defined) consisted mostly of writers and a sprinkling of artists,
musicians and people of the theater. It was a tight community
engaged in endless arguments about what to do to cure Russia
of its horrendous social diseases. They were mercilessly intoler-
ant in these arguments. Their keen affections and equally keen
hatreds for each other were shaped by the sides they took. They
were all ardent Russian patriots, but most of them hated the
czarist autocracy and looked forward to its overthrow.

And there was another group that can be said to belong to
the top *intelligentsia,* but did not belong to the literati-artistic
community. These were the professional revolutionaries. They

devoted their whole life to plotting revolution and preparing for it. It is people from this milieu who led the Bolshevik revolution. It is they who established the dictatorship that ruled the U.S.S.R. for 70 years and led to its death.

But in the beginning no one knew to what the dictatorship would lead. Most people on the left, like my father and later me, cherished fond hopes that eventually dictatorship would dissolve and a people-oriented egalitarian democracy would be established. Father was a believer, and so was I to the very end. But our hopes were shattered and there seemed to be no foundation on which to build a decent society.

I started earning money at age 14. I gave piano lessons to neighborhood kids (almost all girls). I was accompanist for a Hungarian show company, which played operettas (in Hungarian translation) in the industrial suburbs surrounding Chicago where many working class Hungarians lived. The director of the company (he was also the comedian) and his wife (the prima donna) had two children—a boy and a girl. I visited them once and to my delight found that the kids were reading Jules Verne (it was "Captain Grant's Children") in Hungarian translation—my kind of kids. They reminded me of the companionship I was missing.

I was saving money to go to Europe to study music there. The big break came when I won first prize in a piano-playing contest—a grand piano. We sold it for $600. Together with my savings and some support from the philanthropist who sponsored my scholarship in a Chicago music school, I was able to go.

It was only after my five-year stint in Europe and after joining academe back in Chicago that I found my niche. I discovered a culture and a milieu in America where I fit in, a milieu in no way

inferior to the one in Russia that I read about but never partici-
pated in. Even so, I was compelled 30 years ago to leave the
United States for reasons that are stated in my autobiography
(*Certainties and Doubts*. Montreal: Black Rose Books, 2000).

LOOKING BACK

As I wrote *Skating on Thin Ice*, it occurred to me that it was a metaphor for the lives of practically all of my Russian *meshpukhe*.

Take my uncle Niuma, father's younger brother, who went to America with him and stayed when father went back to Russia. Not wanting to lose his Russian citizenship, uncle Niuma came to Russia in the spring of 1914 to register for the peacetime draft. He went back to America some weeks before the First World War broke out, and because he kept his Russian citizenship, he wasn't drafted when the U.S. entered the war in 1917. (The thin ice held.)

Then take my father. He found out that his group would be drafted the day before it was announced on posters in Lozovaya and so was able to leave town. He went to the Caucasus, where the draft was still not in force. When he was a student in the University of Warsaw (evacuated to Rostov), a draft was announced by General Krasnov, who was organizing an army of Don Cossacks to fight the Bolsheviks. Father again escaped (in an open boat) to Crimea. He was mayor of Lozovaya when the Germans occupied it. The German Commander called him in and pointing to his watch announced that if fodder wasn't delivered to his horses within the hour, he would be shot. Fortunately father had horses, hence fodder. The fodder was delivered to the Germans. (The thin ice held.)

And consider father's arrest by the Whites in Crimea on suspicion of contacts with imprisoned Reds. He ventured to disclose to the interrogator that he was indeed a socialist but could not possibly collaborate with the Reds, who shot social democrats as readily as they massacred the Whites. He got away with it. (The thin ice still held.)

Finally, consider the fate of my entire Russian *meshpukhe*. Only two of my maternal grandmother's brothers perished in a pogrom in 1919. *Not one* perished in the Holocaust! All were evacuated to

Author and Gwen Goodrich, newlyweds, 1949

central Asia. Some stayed voluntarily in Siberia. The rest returned to Russia, the Ukraine or Crimea. There are none there now. One cousin-once-removed and her two sons are in Israel, another in Philadelphia, a first cousin and her family in San Francisco. (The ice held once more.)

Author, captain, U.S. Air Force, Alaska 1943

A subordinate theme of this story is my longing for things Russian. Though I had never been in Russia proper, only in conquered lands—Ukraine, Crimea and the Caucasus—I think what I really longed for was to hear Russian speech spoken by real Russians. I finally did—in Alaska, where in 1943–1944 I served as liaison officer with Russian airmen. When some of them brought their families to Nome (where I served), I heard a child speak pure Muscovite Russian. I grieved when she caught scarlet fever and died.

In 1961, immediately after Khruschev's disclosures of Stalin's crimes and the collapse of his cult, I finally got to go to central Russia as a member of a delegation of American psychologists and social scientists. We met colleagues in Moscow, Leningrad, Tbilisi and Tashkent, exchanged views and established ties. The same year I took the family, and we saw most of the Russian *meshpukhe* who had settled in Crimea or gathered there to see us: me—50 years after I left; my wife Gwen (we married in 1949); nine-year-old

Anya; and four-year-old Sasha (Tony wasn't born yet). Among them was my cousin Volodya, who was my first playmate when he was three and I was four and whom I hadn't seen in exactly 50 years. He survived 10 years in the worst arctic concentration camp, Kolyma, as punishment for a careless remark. We started regular intense correspondence, which lasted until his death in 1998.

From then on I went to Russia every two or three years to conferences or by invitation of research institutes or universities. With one in particular, the Institute of System Research, I exchanged many translations of articles from English to Russian and vice-versa. On my last visit, I was thrilled to see Russian translations of three of my books. I had known about these translations but was previously not allowed to see them. The books were then still on

Author's American meshpukhe in 1940.
Author seated first on left in first row; directly to his right, Uncle Niuma;
immediately above him, his parents.

the restricted list, available only to Communist Party members. With the advent of *glasnost* (essentially freedom not only to write but also to read) they could be shown to me. As of this writing, my book *Conversations with Three Russians,* which I wrote in Russian, is at Progress-Traditsia publishing house.

My last visit was a few months before the Soviet Union imploded. The results, as everyone knows, were horrendous. So again I felt lucky. My ardent wish to see the country of my birth was granted just at the time when she was recovering from seven decades of bloody tyranny and just short of the chaos that followed its collapse. By then not one of my Russian *meshpukhe* was in Russia. For them, as for me, the thin ice held all the way.

GLOSSARY

absentee owner: Owner of a large tract of farmland who generally lives elsewhere and leaves the management to hired professionals. In czarist Russia many of the aristocracy or gentry were absentee owners, sometimes of several estates, and lived on incomes from them.

arshin (Russian): A measure of length in czarist Russia. 1 *arshin* = 28 inches.

autocracy: A form of government where all power resides in a single person. In a monarchy, it is usually a king, in Russia, the czar or emperor. The emperor called himself "Autocrat of all the Russias." After World War I there were no autocratic monarchies in Europe, but many dictatorships appeared, in which all power was concentrated in a single person—the dictator. Mussolini of Italy, Stalin of the Soviet Union, Hitler of Germany were the most prominent dictators (that is, non-royal autocrats) between the two world wars.

Baku: A large city on the Caspian Sea, the center of the Russian oil industry. In the Soviet era, Baku became the capital of Azerbaijan, one of the 15 Soviet republics, now an independent state. Its present population is given as five million.

barricade: In the 20th century, several (mostly unsuccessful) revolutions broke out in European cities. Soldiers were sent in to break up the demonstrations. The revolutionaries often tried to block the troops sent against them by building barriers in the streets (overturned streetcars, piles of stones or bricks, etc.). These barricades were scenes of violent encounters between the revolutionaries and the police or military.

Bolshevik (Russian): In czarist Russia there were two major socialist (which see) political parties (both illegal until 1906). The Social Democratic Party was concerned mainly with the plight of workers in mills, factories, mines, etc. The Social Revolutionary Party was concerned mainly with the plight of the peasants. In 1903, the Social Democratic Party split into two factions—the Bolsheviks and the Mensheviks. The Bolsheviks were more radical. They believed that socialism could be established only by a revolution. After the czarist government was overthrown, they insisted that Russia sign a separate peace with Germany. The Mensheviks believed that socialism could be established only gradually by democratically sanctioned measures.

bulrushes: Plants growing in wetlands or near banks of rivers.

Caucasian mountains: A compact mountain range separating North Caucasus from Transcaucasia, a sort of a backbone of the region between the Black and the Caspian seas; site of bitter wars between Russians and warlike Moslem tribes, something like the wars against Native Americans in the West. Russia's greatest writer, Leo Tolstoy, and the two greatest poets, Alexander Pushkin and Yuri Lermontov, wrote much about the Caucasus and its peoples.

certificate of maturity: Diploma issued upon successful completion of the course of study prescribed by the *gymnasia*.

Cherkassy: Town on the Dnieper River in the Kiev *gubernia*. Author's mother's birthplace.

classics: In literature, books that, unlike most of today's best sellers, are read by many generations sometimes for centuries, such as the novels of Dickens, Tolstoy, Balzac or Mark Twain, or Shakespeare's plays; in music, works of great composers, especially of the 18th and 19th centuries—Bach, Mozart, Beethoven, Schubert.

communists: Originally, people who believed that eventually all private property will be abolished in human society, that everything will belong to every one jointly. Communists believed that people will work because they will want to serve the commonweal rather than for pay or for profits. They believed that people will be given free of charge everything that they may need or require, so money will be abolished. In the Middle Ages, monasteries were established as "communes" based on these principles. In our day some religious sects have established communities of this sort. The *kibbutzim* (the collective farms of Israel) are another example. In the United States and other affluent countries, communism has been firmly associated with the authoritarian system established in the Soviet Union, particularly the absolute dictatorship of the Communist Party or of its leader.

Constituent Assembly: A body to be convened for framing a constitution for Russia after the overthrow of the monarchy. The assembly convened in January 1918 but was dissolved by the Bolshevik government the day after the first meeting.

Cossacks: Auxiliary troops in the czarist military establishment (practically all cavalry), who originally lived on Russia's border lands guarding the country from invaders and marauders. They were given lands and privileges and eventually became a force fiercely loyal to the czar. Cossacks were frequently used by the czarist government in quelling riots and revolutionary demonstrations.

Crimea: Peninsula extending from the northern coast of the Black Sea; scene of the Crimean War (1853-56) waged against Russia by England, France and Turkey primarily to prevent Russia's expansion at Turkey's cost and free access by Russia's navy into the Mediterranean Sea. The "Charge of the Light Brigade" glorified by Tennyson ("Theirs not to question why; theirs but to do and die...") was a battle in that war. Author's last home in Russia.

demi-monde (French): Literally "half world." In 18th-century Europe, high society (the rich, the titled, the famous) were called "the world." A woman who, because of her wealth, brilliance, sophistication would be of the "world," except for her questionable morals was said to belong to the "half world." Violetta, the heroine of Verdi's opera *La Traviata,* was a *demi-mondaine,* that is, belonging to the *demi-monde.*

Denikin: A general of the White Army who made the most extensive gains against the Soviets in 1919 but was repulsed almost at the gates of Moscow. His army consisting largely of czarist officers disintegrated.

Don Cossacks: The Cossacks were given lands along the frontiers of Russia in the 16th century when it was "Muscovy." The land given to these were alongside the River Don. Rostov-on-

Don is the principal city of the region. The Don Cossacks lost to the Bolsheviks. Many emigrated. Some who were outstanding singers organized the Don Cossack choir, which became famous in the West in the period between the two world wars.

dynasty: In most monarchies, the eldest son or daughter of the monarch succeeds upon the death of the monarch. If there are no children, usually the closest relative succeeds. The dynasty lasts as long as the throne is kept in the family. There were just two dynasties in czarist Russia, that of Rurik, the first prince, a Viking, and the Romanov dynasty. The 300th anniversary of this dynasty was celebrated in 1913, just four years before it ended.

excommunication: A person excommunicated from the Russian Orthodox or from the Roman Catholic church is denied the sacraments (marriage, confession, funeral). In Russia the excommunicated person could not be mentioned in any publication (became an "unperson.") Leo Tolstoy was excommunicated in his old age for refusing to believe in the dogmas of the Russian Orthodox Church (divinity of Jesus, virginity of Mary, etc.)

external study: Studying outside a school.

February revolution: The overthrow of the Russian monarchy in 1917.

ghetto: Originally, quarters in most European cities to which Jews were confined until well into the 20th century. When the Germans occupied Poland in 1939, the Warsaw ghetto was turned into a concentration camp. In 1943, the Jews revolted and fought the Germans with improvised weapons. Almost all were massacred and the ghetto was razed. A monument stands on the site commemorating the tragedy.

Gogol: The second great figure of Russian 19th century literature (Pushkin was the first).

gubernia (Russian): A district of the Russian empire corresponding roughly to a state of the U.S. or a province of Canada but with far less autonomy (self government).

gymnasia (Russian): Secondary school in czarist Russia.

Hades: According to the beliefs of ancient Greeks, the abode of the dead.

Hebrew: Language spoken by ancient Jews. Most of the Old Testament was written in Hebrew. When the state of Israel was established in 1948, a modernized form of Hebrew became its official language

heder (Yiddish-Hebrew): Elementary Jewish School. Practically all Jewish children in czarist Russia attended a *heder*. In consequence there was no illiteracy among Russian Jews. This does not mean that they all were literate in Russian. Attaining literacy in Russian was the first step toward a secular education among young Russian Jews.

hussar: a mounted soldier of a crack cavalry unit armed with a sabre.

icon: In Russia, a painting of a saint, usually an object of worship.

izvozchik (Russian): A horse-drawn cab.

Kharkov: A large city north of Lozovaya, capital of a *gubernia* of that name.

khazr (Hebrew-Yiddish): pork.

Kasrilevka: Fictional *stetl* in the works of Sholom Aleichem, the foremost writer in Yiddish.

Kiev: A large city on the Dnieper River, capital of a *gubernia* of that name.

kipiatok (Russian): Boiling water. During long railway journeys, Russians loved to drink tea. When the train stopped in stations, they went to the buffet, carrying tea kettles to be filled with *kipiatok* that they took back to the cars, where they brewed the tea (which they had brought along). Tea drinking in Russia was usually a social occasion. Railroad cars were not like our buses, where people sit behind other people's backs. A compartment on a passenger train was like a room. People could sit facing each other and engage in endless conversations—a favorite Russian and Russian-Jewish pastime.

konka (Russian): A horse-drawn street car.

kopek (Russian): 1 ruble = 100 kopeks.

kulturnost (Russian): Being well informed and well mannered.

Lenin (1870-1924): Revolutionary alias of Vladimir Ilyich Ulianov, leader of the Bolshevik faction of the Russian Social Democratic Party, founder of the Soviet Union

Lozovaya: A town south of Kharkov in what is now Ukraine. The Russian Encyclopedic Dictionary lists Lozovaya as a town with population (1991) 71,000, five times as large as at the time of the author's birth.

Makhno: Anarchist guerrilla leader in the 1918-21 civil war, at first allied with the Bolsheviks, then fighting against them. Noted for his ferocity, especially against the Jews.

matzoth: Unleavened bread, eaten instead of bread during Passover, to commemorate hurried exodus from Egypt. (There was no time to the dough to leaven.)

melamed (Hebrew-Yiddish): Teacher in an elementary Hebrew school.

Menshevik (Russian): See Bolshevik.

meshpukhe (Yiddish-Hebrew): Extended family including distant cousins, uncles, aunts, their in-laws, etc. In czarist Russia contact was usually kept up and get-togethers were arranged on special occasions (weddings, etc.).

NEP: New Economic Policy. In 1921, the Communists who ruled Russia retreated somewhat from the policy of "war communism," under which all private trade was strictly prohibited. The appearance of legal markets relieved starvation that had spread all over Soviet Russia.

October revolution: The overthrow of the Provisional Government of Russia in 1917.

Odessa: Russian navy base on the Black Sea; scene of an extensive mutiny of sailors in 1905.

Petlura: Leader of Ukrainian nationalist forces in the 1918-21 civil war. Fought both the Reds and the Whites.

pince-nez (French): Literally "nose-pinch." Glasses held by a clasp on the nose. They were regarded as more dignified than the glasses worn today, held by shafts stretching to behind the ears. The *pince-nez* could easily fall off; therefore a string was attached to them, as can be seen in pictures of prominent people of the time.

pogrom: Violent riot, often organized by government agencies in czarist Russia, aimed at Jews, who were beaten up, sometimes killed.

Provisional Government: In Russia, the government formed after the overthrow of the monarchy, which was to rule Russia until the country's political form was decided by a Constituent Assembly.

quota: A share allotted in a distribution. Here, quota is the percent of Jewish applicants admitted to a gymnasia or a university, namely 3 percent. The *Encyclopedia Britannica* (Eleventh Edition) lists the population of Russia in 1904 as 149 million, of which five million were Jews. That is, about 3.3% of the population were Jews. Thus a quota of 3% appeared "fair," if one does not take into account that a much larger percent of the Jewish population applied for admission to gymnasia, or that a much larger percentage of the population were Jews in regions where Jews were permitted to live.

Reds: In the Russian civil war (1918-1921), the armed forces of the Bolsheviks.

revolutionary: In czarist Russia, a person dedicated to the overthrow of the czarist regime, usually a member of a secret organization (some, but not all, terrorist) with this aim.

Rostov-on-Don: A city on the River Don, near its mouth at the Sea of Azov. Principal city of the region populated by the Don Cossacks. Their lifestyle and prominent role in the civil war of 1918-21 were vividly described in Sholokhov's novel *And Quiet Flows the Don*. The University of Warsaw, which was attended by the author's father, was evacuated to Rostov-on-Don, when the Germans occupied Warsaw in 1915.

ruble: The Russian monetary unit. In czarist Russia 1 ruble was equal to 50 cents U.S. Since the revolution its value fluctuated wildly.

secular: As in secular education, as distinguished from religious education. The Jews, especially those living in Eastern Europe, were strongly devoted to religious education, that is, to the study of the Bible and other writings directly or indirectly related to religion. Science (physics, chemistry, biology) and what is called humanities (history, literature, the arts) had no place in the sort of education that pious Jews revered. When young people in Russia started to aspire to professional life (which demanded knowledge provided by secular education) it was natural for them to become estranged from religion. This is what the generation gap among the Jews of that time was about.

seder: ceremonial meal celebrating the exodus of Jews from Egypt.

serf: Usually a peasant who is fixed to the land belonging to a landlord. Unlike a slave, a serf could not be readily bought and sold, separated from his or her family, etc. But he could not leave the landlord's domain, and when the estate was sold, the serf went with the estate. In Russia most peasants were serfs until 1861, when they were liberated by Czar Alexander II.

socialists: People who believe that business enterprises, especially very large ones, large tracts of land and natural resources should belong to everyone, not just to investors, and managed by agencies of the government, provided it is a democratic one, responsible to the people who elected it.

Soviet: Literally a council (the Russian word *soviet* means advice). During the first (aborted) revolution of 1905, soviets of workers' and peasants' deputies were established to provide guidelines for the course of the revolution. They were dissolved when the revolution failed and reconvened in 1917 after the overthrow of the czarist government. When the Bolsheviks overthrew the provisional government in November 1917, all authority supposedly was vested in the soviets. Soon, however, the Bolsheviks excluded members of all parties from the soviets except their own. Eventually, the soviets became rubber stamp bodies. The Soviet Union was ruled by the leaders of the Bolshevik faction (which was renamed the Communist Party). Finally, these, too were purged (mostly shot) when Joseph Stalin became the absolute dictator of the country.

Stalin: Revolutionary alias of Iosif Vissarionovich Djugashvili, a native of Georgia (a country in the Caucasus) who joined the Bolsheviks and became a member of the ruling group after the October revolution. After Lenin's death, he gradually acquired more and more power, until he became the absolute ruler. He had practically all of Lenin's closest associates shot to prevent any challenge to his absolute power (See Lenin).

stetl (Yiddish): Literally a little town. In czarist Russia, most Jews could live legally only in a designated area in the southwest corner of the empire. Since they could not own land, they could not live in the country, so they huddled in the usually impoverished *stetls*.

verst (Russian): 3,500 feet (about 2/3 of a mile).

Viking: Originally the word meant sea pirate, which was indeed a principal occupation of Scandinavian tribes in the Middle Ages.

Whites: In the Russian civil war 1918-21, armed forces fighting against the Reds. Also called the White Guard.

Wrangel: The last of the White generals.

Yehupetz: Fictional city in the works of Sholom Aleichem; a pseudonym of Kiev.

Yiddish: Language spoken by Jews in czarist Russia, Poland and eastern parts of the Austro-Hungarian empire. It is derived from German and, except for the Hebrew words in its vocabulary, is easily understood by German speakers. Vice versa, speakers of Yiddish easily understand German. Unlike other European languages, Yiddish is written with Hebrew characters and reads like Arabic, from right to left.

TIME LINE

1905   January 5 (Old Style), January 22 (New Style): Bloody Sunday.

1905   Russian revolution (crushed in 1906).

1906   Author's father and younger brother go to America.

1907   Author's father returns to Russia.

1910   March 19 (Old Style), April 1 (New Style): Author's parents marry.

1911   May 9 (Old Style), May 22 (New Style): Author born in Lozovaya.

1915   September: Author's father leaves for Baku to escape the draft.

1915   Author and his mother move in with mother's family.

1916   March: Author and his mother leave for Baku.

1916   November: Author's father admitted to university (Faculty of Law) in Rostov-on-Don.

1916   November: Author and his mother return to Lozovaya.

1916   December: Author begins music lessons.

1917 February (Old style), March (New Style): Monarchy overthrown.

1917 August: Author and his mother ill with typhoid fever.

1917 October (Old Style), November (New Style): October revolution.

1918 January: Constituent Assembly meets and is dissolved by the Bolsheviks.

1918 March: Author and his mother leave for Feodosia in the Crimea.

1918 May: Germans occupy Crimea.

1918 November: Author and his mother return to Lozovaya.

1918 Author's father escapes the draft into General Krasnov's army; his whereabouts are unknown.

Winter 1918-1919 Civil war rages in the Ukraine. Lozovaya occupied by the Reds, then by the Whites, then by roving guerrilla bands. Jews usually the targeted victims of plunder.

Spring 1919: Reds control most of Ukraine and Crimea. Travel becomes possible. Author's father turns out to be in Crimea. Author and his mother rejoin him there.

Summer 1919: Whites reconquer southern Ukraine and Crimea. Western allies against Germany support the Whites. Feodosia becomes a boom town. Author's father and partner run a leather store. Author's family becomes prosperous. Author continues music lessons, also French and English lessons.

Winter 1919-1920: Reds reconquer Ukraine.

1920: Most Western navies leave the Black Sea. Whites bottled up in Crimea.

1920: November. Reds break through the fortifications in Perekop on the isthmus between Crimea and mainland. Whites flee to Constantinople. Those left behind are killed by the Reds in mass executions.

Winter 1920-1921: Starvation in Crimea. Father goes to work in the Department of Education.

1921   April: Author's father gets a month's leave of absence. Family returns to Lozovaya, where food is plentiful.

1921   May: At author's mother's insistence, author's father decides not to return to Feodosia. The family leaves for the stetl on the Russian-Polish border.

1921   September: Author's mother crosses border illegally, gets to Warsaw and contacts relatives in Chicago. Makes arrangements for emigrating to America.

1921   December: Author's mother returns to village on the Polish side of the border. A smuggler delivers her note to father, informing him that she is waiting for him to cross. The smuggler brings author and his father to a hideout on the bank of the river, where they wait for an opportunity to cross. After several days of futile waiting, author attempts to cross the river on skates, is threatened by a border guard and returns back to the Russian side. Finally the smuggler arrives with a bribed Red Army man, who shows where to cross the river. Author and his father walk across the ice at night and are reunited with his mother.

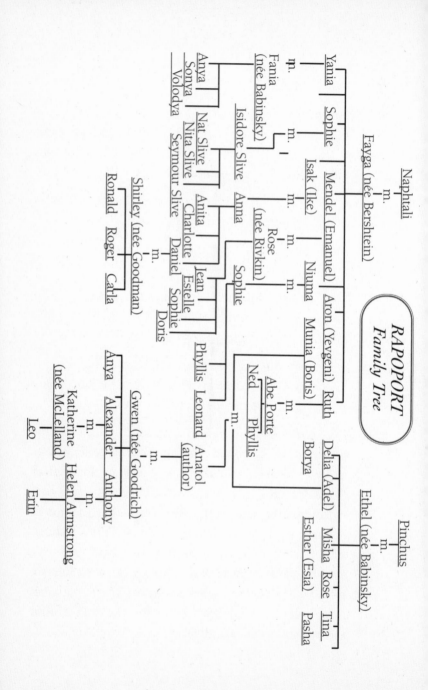

RAPOPORT
Family Tree

184

ABOUT THE AUTHOR

Anatol Rapoport is currently Professor Emeritus of Psychology at the University of Toronto. His scholarly interests cover a broad range of topics. He has published numerous influential books and articles on philosophy, psychology, decision theory and peace studies. He was selected as Fellow at the Center for Advanced Studies in the Behavioral Sciences and the American Academy of Arts and Sciences. He is recipient of the Lenz International Peace Research Prize, the Comprehensive Achievement Award of the Society for General Systems Research and the Harold J. Lasswell Award for Distinguished Scientific Contributions to Political Psychology.

ANATOL RAPOPORT

Vita

Born May 22, 1911, Lozovaya, Russia.

Citizenship: U.S.A., Landed Immigrant in Canada since 1973.

Married, three children born in 1952, 1957, 1962.

Education: Chicago public schools, 1922-1929; Staatsakademie für Musik und darstellende Kunst, Vienna, 1929-1934; University of Chicago, 1937-1941, B.S. 1938, M.S. 1940, Ph.D. (Mathematics), 1941.

Military service: U.S. Air Force, 1942-1946, lieutenant, then captain.

Academic Positions

Instructor of mathematics, Illinois Institute of Technology, 1946-1947.

Research Associate, then Assistant Professor, Committee on Mathematical Biology, University of Chicago, 1947-1954.

Associate Professor, then Professor and Senior Research Mathematician, Mental Health Research Institute, University of Michigan, 1955-1970.

Professor of Psychology and Mathematics, University of Toronto, 1970-1980.

Director, Institut für Höhere Studien, Vienna, 1980-1984.

Professor of Peace and Conflict Studies, University of Toronto, 1984-96.

Professor Emeritus of Psychology, University of Toronto, 1996—present

Guest Professorships

University of Warsaw, 1961-1962.

Institut für Höhere Studien, Vienna, 1968.

Technical University of Denmark, 1968-1969.

Institut für Höhere Studien, Vienna, 1976-77.

Wissenschaftszentrum, Berlin, 1978.

University of Hiroshima, 1978.

University of Mannheim, 1988.

University of Munich, 1989.

University of Bern, summers 1991-1999.

Editorial

Editor, *General Systems*; Associate Editor, *Journal of Conflict Resolution, Behavioral Science, ETC.: A Review of General Semantics*. Member of Editorial Boards of about 10 journals.

Honors and Awards

Fellow, Center for Advanced Studies in the Behavioral Sciences, 1954-1955; Fellow, American Academy of Arts and Sciences, 1960—present; Doctor of Humane Letters (hon.), University of Western Michigan, 1971; Lenz International Peace Research Prize, 1975; Society for General Systems Research Comprehensive Achievement Award, 1983; Doctor of Laws (hon.), University of Toronto, 1986; Harold D. Lasswell Award for Distinguished Scientific Contributions to Political Psychology, 1986; Doctor of Science (hon.), Royal Military College, 1995, Ehrendoktor, University of Bern, 1997.

Publications

Books:

Science and the Goals of Man, 1950

Operational Philosophy, 1953

Fights, Games, and Debates, 1960

Strategy and Conscience, 1964

Prisoner's Dilemma (with A.M. Chammah), 1965

Two-Person Game Theory, 1966

N-Person Game Theory, 1970

The Big Two, 1971

Conflict in Man-made Environment, 1974

Semantics, 1975

The 2 x 2 Game (with M. Geyer and D. Gordon), 1976

Mathematics Methoden in den Socialwissenschaften, 1983

Mathematical Methods in the Social and Behavioral Sciences, 1984

General System Theory, 1986

The Origins of Violence, 1989 (Revised edition, 1995)

Decision Theory and Decision Behavior, 1989 (Revised edition, 1998)

Canada and the World (with Anthony Rapoport), 1992

Peace, an Idea Whose Time Has Come, 1993

Gewißheiten und Zweifel, 1994

Uverenost i somnienia, 1999

Certainties and Doubts, 2000

Edited Volumes and Translations:

Clausewitz, C. von, *On War*, 1968

Game Theory as a Theory of Conflict Resolution, 1974

The Structure of Awareness, translation of *Kofliktuyushchie Struktury* by V.A. Lefebvre, 1977

Non-antagonistic Games, translation of *Igry s Nieprotivopolozhnymi*
   Interesami by Yu. B. Germeier, 1986
Journal articles (about 400)
Entries in encyclopedias (about 10)
Chapters contributed to books (about 40)

Memberships
American Mathematical Society; Society for Mathematical
Biology; International Soceity for General Semantics (president
1953-1955); Society for General Systems Research (president
1965-1966); Canadian Peace Research and Education Association
(president 1972-1975); Science for Peace (president 1984-1986).